# ENGLISH IN ASIA

E.P.L. - CPL

**John Wharton**

Additional copies of <u>English in Asia</u> are available for US$12.95. <u>Jobs in Japan--the Complete Guide to Living and Working in Japan</u> (276pp) is available for US$14.95. Please add $2 surface postage (worldwide), $3 1st Class postage (US or Canada) or $5 airmail (overseas) per order. Non-US orders, please use postal money order or US bank check. Volume discounts available. Allow two weeks for delivery.

Address orders and correspondence to:

**The Global Press**
697 College Parkway
Rockville MD 20850 USA
Tel. (202)466-1663

ISBN 0-911285-03-2

Printed in the United States of America

First Edition

NOTE: While every attempt has been made to ensure the accuracy of this information, changes in government policy and institutional operations make mistakes inevitable. Please confirm all essential facts independently before making major decisions. The Global Press assumes no responsibility for damages resulting from the use of the information contained herein.

# Contents

# Introduction

Although the current economic woes of Western English speaking countries are well-known and much-discussed these days, one legacy of "The British Century" (the 19th) and "The American Century" (our 20th) remains undiminished: our common language is the world's most widely spoken. Mandarin Chinese is certainly the most widely-spoken *native* language but today, well over one billion people are estimated to have at least a fair command of English and, with the collapse of Communism, the number stands to grow exponentially as former colonies seek to plug themselves into the world community. *Do svidania, Rooski,* hello English.

There is no question that the need today for English teachers has never been higher but, as with any kind of employment, opportunities vary according to location. Of course, it is possible to teach foreign students in your native America, Canada, UK or Australia but there you will be facing the stiff competition of experienced instructors willing to work for relatively low domestic wages. This book, on the other hand, is for you who have the initiative and drive to go direct to where the prime teaching opportunities are today: the wealthy and dynamic Asian countries of Japan, Korea and Taiwan.

There are those people (some foreign, but mostly native speakers) who say there's something slightly unseemly about a person teaching English who gained the gift of that valuable language by dint of birth rather than struggle in the classroom. Perhaps all of us English as a Foreign Language (EFL) teachers have wrestled with some small bit of—what, guilt?—at how very well we effortlessly speak the language our students anguish over every day in our classrooms.

But such is the situation in Asia and the sad fact is that English is one tough nut to crack, especially when the cracker comes from a linguistic background as alien as Japanese, Korean or Chinese. Sure we native speakers are darned lucky to have been born in a land where English is the dominant language but that's Lady Luck for you. The next time you hear a student bemoaning his bad luck at not having been born to English, remind him that it works both ways. Just have him ask a foreigner trying to learn to speak *his* language how fortunate *he* feels!

So, as Woody Allen might put it, enough with the guilt already. You, as a native English speaker blessed with the world language as your mother tongue, are just what the millions and millions of Asian students of our language think they need to "internationalize" (the current buzzword of choice in Asia). And, as you've probably learned either first-hand, from friends or from my guidebook, JOBS IN JAPAN, the people of the Orient are very eager to have you teach them what you never had to learn.

Easy money? Well, although the pay can be very good for English teachers (in Japan ranging to $80 an hour just to chat with a businessman), most of the work requires preparation, extreme concentration and just plain energy. You'll earn every *yen, won* or *kuai* you make in the classroom, believe me!

I'm often asked by those preparing for the jaunt to Japan and the Little Dragons of Asia, "How long can this English-mania last? Surely someday another language will supplant "King English" or the Orientals will just lose interest. And what about the many native speakers already going over, especially to Japan? Won't they toughen the competition?"

In response, I always encourage the inquirer to look, for example, to the Japanese culture for the answer. Since earliest times, Japanese have always followed the current leader. They are a generally humble folk who have a very realistic view of their place in the world: a small island nation full of industrious people--and not much else.

As such, they know that they are destined to ride on bigger coattails than their own. Hundreds of years ago, those coattails belonged to China, from whom they imported their entire writing system. The biggest coattails to be seen today, however, are still America's, a gargantuan country (despite all the gloom-and-doom chatter in the popular press) that won't soon be losing its "de facto" dominance.

The sheer size and wealth of the Anglophone countries of America, Canada, the UK, Ireland, Australia and New Zealand make them (especially the US) the logical focus of Asia's energies. Just as feudal lords sought to increase their wealth by getting close to the emperor, so Asia seeks to be ever closer to America and the whole English-speaking world. For it is the 700,000,000 inhabitants of that world who control the vast majority of the planet's wealth and it is that wealth that Asia would like a part of and knows its well-being depends on.

The concern about an oversupply of English teachers in Japan is perhaps a more valid one. True, more native speakers are going there to try their hand as *sensei* but the numbers are still minuscule. Immigration's best estimate is only around 8,000 currently to which must be added a large number of *gaijin* teaching on either a cultural ("student") visa, special work-related visa or illegally as tourists.

Contrast that number (perhaps 10,000 foreigners) with an estimate made by *The Wall Street Journal* that as many as 10,000,000 adult Japanese may be currently enrolled in or looking for English conversation classes, most of which are taught by foreign instructors. I believe it's very safe to say that there are at least 1,000 Japanese looking for your services as a *sensei*, a number which even if cut in half would still be more work than you could accept.

No doubt, competition exists in the major cities of Japan but elsewhere in that country and throughout Korea and Taiwan, the need for native speaker English teachers is nowhere near being met. As the latter countries leave the Third World and move into the ranks of true industrial powers, their English demands are growing faster than the supply of teachers on this side of the world can respond. Don't worry, the work *is* available and, given the high turnover rate among teachers and booming economies of Asia, you're liable to be *more* in demand in the coming years, not *less.*

But what is the English teacher to the Asian student? Most involved in the industry would have to admit that actually teaching English is only a part of what a good teacher does in the classroom. The "affective" (emotional) components of the job are every bit as critical for successful instruction as getting the right response in drill.

You'll find that the vast majority of Oriental students of our language are terribly intent on learning it and work very hard at its study. More than a few of the adults you'll teach will be somewhat disheartened at having worked so hard for so many years only to find themselves unable to carry on a meaningful conversation with you. But learning to actually speak a foreign language (especially when the student's earlier focus has been on writing and reading) takes patience and practice.

For this reason, a big part of teaching will involve motivating and encouraging, whether the object of your attention is a ten-year-old who can't quite believe the noise you make is really a language or a gray-topped company president trying to share tidbits of corporate trivia with you. They'll all want to talk to you and it'll be up to you to help them do so naturally.

Your students, it should be remembered, may not be the most demonstrative people in their support of your efforts but, almost without exception, they really want you to succeed with them. For it is only by your success that they will have the whole world of opportunity that English represents open for them.

Helping anyone attain such a sought-after goal is a very large responsibility and it's my hope that by telling you something about our language and how best to practice our profession, you'll bring the kind of enthusiasm and concern to the classroom that the finest teachers seem to be able to summon up at will. With professional pride and care, you too can give the gift of our language to your students. And if that prospect gives you a bit of a warm, fuzzy feeling, then you'll probably make a pretty good teacher!

# The Development of Language

Consider if you will the humble bumble (bee, that is). Industrious, gregarious, gracious enough to share with us his wonderfully tasty regurgitations of the day's pollen-gathering. Yes, man has much to admire about this prickly paradigm of our own society. But there's one quality about the bee that may make him our very closest kinsman in all the animal realm. Amazingly enough, the bee and man are the only two creatures on the planet that we know to be capable of non-contiguous communication. In other words, only we two beasties can tell our species of things happening outside the immediate area of communication.

Now, there may be those who resent having Shakespeare's sonnets compared to the animated wiggling of a drone trying to tell his hive of an especially appealing poinsettia but there is no other animal we know of that can convey information to its own kind about things outside where the "conversation" takes place. Lions roar, whales sing, dogs bark and they all qualify as a kind of language...but, as far as we know, only barely.

For the record, a language is simply "a system of arbitrary symbols by means of which a social group cooperates," at least according to linguist Bernard Bloch. In fact, language seems ready-made for man. Once our species decided to stand upright, we were relieved of having to hold our breath while using our arms for locomotion. On two legs, our relatively highly-placed vocal apparatus (tongue, vocal cords, jaw, teeth) is very well-suited to throwing a great number of distinct noises quite far.

Oddly enough, the primates, although blessed with more-or-less the same apparatus as ours, have no more instinctive language than any other animal. Only the parrot, with its keen ear for imitation, can even *sound* like it's communicating although it's totally incapable of original language.

Tightening the vocal cords causes a rise in pitch, which the Chinese and Scandinavians (among others) use to give the same word different meanings. Not allowing the vocal cords to vibrate is whispering, common to all languages. By positioning the tongue, teeth and uvula in the back of the throat, humans can make an astonishing number of distinct and regularly reproducible sounds, almost all of which have meaning in some language somewhere.

But perhaps the most amazing feature of language is its infinite variety. The vast majority of utterances we encounter have never been heard by us before and yet we understand them, usually perfectly. There is no area of experience that is incommunicable (as long as the parties are willing to invest the time to explain) and there is no idea that can't be conveyed by those intent on its communication.

If you've been feeling somewhat intimidated by the speed and agility of today's computers, just ask an engineer about voice-recognition in his machine and how it compares to our own ability to understand almost any other speaker of our language talking about almost any subject. If he's honest, he'll tell you that even today's multi-million dollar silicon speedsters can't comprehend one-tenth the variety of voices and ideas the human mind can. (And, from what I understand, only the most sophisticated can dance around to tell other computers where especially delicious voltage can be found!)

Writing of all kinds apparently developed from picture signs: literal depictions of objects and actions. The Chinese and Japanese still use these "pictographs" (the Chinese use them exclusively, the Japanese in conjunction with two home-grown alphabets) but other cultures have developed more abstract forms to relieve the pictographs' tremendous strain on human memory.

The Greeks invented the first true alphabet by using consonantal characters in Phoenician script for which no sounds existed in Greek to represent vowels in their own language. From this Greek alphabet came the Cyrillic alphabet (used in Slavic languages, including Russian) and our own Roman alphabet.

Of course, as languages developed in small pockets of civilization, variations also developed. Dialects formed within linguistic populations too large to maintain a single form of speech, often as the result of influences from other languages. Still, speakers of these dialects could easily understand each other except when the number of dialects grew extreme.

That's just what happened in Europe before the advent of telecommunications. Such a great number of dialects developed on the Continent that, for example, residents near the French-Roman frontier were at one time unintelligible by the residents of their respective capitals. The dialects could be understood by others immediately contiguous to the area and those contiguous dialects were understood by *their* neighbors but distant dialects may as well have been entirely different languages.

When distant trading became common, natives and foreign merchants alike needed to develop some common form of communication between their two alien societies. The "pidgin" languages that used bits and pieces of both languages (and sometimes a common third language as well) were purely economic tools that allowed the native producer and the foreign trader to dicker effectively on matters of business.

If trade were substantial enough and a particular pidgin became common enough to be passed on to later generations as their *first* language, the pidgin became a "Creole". Haitian Creole, for example, shows lexical and grammatical structures from French and several African languages.

Much to the frustration of language teachers, no one is quite certain how even the dimmest member of a culture is able to learn his mother language as it is spoken in his immediate environment. But somehow, it's a gift every member of a society (regardless of genetic makeup) is given.

First-language acquisition occurs at a rapid pace and without apparent effort by a process called "grammar construction"--basically just trial and error usage of words and phrases heard around them. At the end of their first year, babies enlarge upon their repertoire of dozens of consistent (and highly effective!) pre-verbal communications and start making attempts to imitate words they hear around them. They will probably send their parents into fits of ecstasy at this stage by uttering their first "word", often just a misinterpreted belch.

By 18 months, the infant language student is stringing words together in two and three-word "sentences"--usually called "telegraphic" utterances due to their simple and effective content. By age three, he can chatter incessantly. (Long gone is the parents' delight at hearing him speak!)

By the time English-speaking children reach four, they can easily form plurals, the present progressive, past tense, third-person singular and possessives. (One study by linguist Jean Berko found that a child of that age would conjugate the false word "gling" into "glinged" and sometimes "glang," suggesting a very sophisticated understanding of past tense formation.)

Behaviorists like B.F. Skinner believe that we learn by "operant conditioning", that is, the child "operates" language to get what it desires. And if "want milk" makes Mom bring the good stuff, the lesson is learned. The biggest problem with this theory, however, is the simple fact that most of what we say is completely new and therefore unproven in operational effectiveness.

The great linguist, Noam Chomsky, was among those who suggested that we have within us the innate capacity to learn language and that we are biologically programmed to learn a language by a "Language Acquisition Device" or LAD. This LAD allows us to distinguish speech sounds from other environmental noise and construct the simplest possible system of language out of the language samples around us.

Whatever it is that allows us to so easily and readily learn our first language sadly disappears more or less at puberty. Although the difficulty of second-language learning has traditionally been blamed on "interference" with the first language, in fact, multi-linguals ("polyglots") really *can* learn several languages equally well and easily if they do so at a young age.

What seems more important in explaining the vastly increased difficulty we experience in learning a language in adulthood is what neurolinguistic scientists are starting to term "lateralization" of the brain. An ongoing process from birth, this phenomenon is essentially an unconscious assigning of tasks by the individual to one side of the brain or the other.

As the child matures, the left hemisphere usually becomes increasingly dominant, emphasizing the analytical and intellectual aspects of the mind. It is thought by many adherents of the lateralization theory that once this dominance of the intellectual over the emotional side occurs, we tend to overanalyze and not be "free" enough in our efforts to learn a second language. Whereas children learn their first language almost by a kind of osmosis, it's possible that adult second language learners have become too rigid to just "go with the flow" in order to learn as easily as their infantile counterparts.

# The Evolution of English

Luckily for us, we were able to master English before our LADs went bad. Because ours is such an exceptionally difficult language to learn with its many diverse linguistic influences, some foreigners may believe that we native speakers are a race of geniuses for being able to speak their target of intense study with such facility. Most students of our language, however, know that our command of the language was just plain dumb luck--the luck of having been born the descendants of nomads chasing woolly mammoths around the plains of southeast Europe about 5,000 years ago.

It was these nomads who spoke the granddaddy of English: Proto-Indo-European. From this proto-English, came (among such other exotics as Hindi and Sanskrit) three Germanic forms: East (now extinct), North (which evolved into the Scandinavian languages) and West (which became German, Dutch and, much later, English).

A major reason for the complexity of English is that it has been shaped by numerous invaders of the British Isles, each interweaving their own language into the existing amalgam. Among the earliest such conquerors were the Romans who occupied much of the islands, adding Latin in pre-Christian days to the native Celtic. Then, in the fifth and sixth centuries, Saxons, Jutes and Frisians crossed to England from Denmark and northern Germany. Along with them came the tribe that would come to name the country and our language: the Angles, named after an "angle" or corner of land between Schleswig and Flensburg near the German-Danish border.

After depositing such delightful peculiarities into the language as the mutated plurals *feet, geese, teeth, men, women, lice* and *mice,* the Germanic tribes were conquered by the Vikings who left us many down-to-earth words including *nay* for *no* and *fro* for *from.* The modern language closest to the Old English of that time is to be found in Iceland today.

In the 12th and 13th centuries, after the French invasion, there was actually a chance that English would die out all together as the French conquerors dominated British politics, science and the arts. Fortunately (perhaps unfortunately in the eyes of some students of the language), events sustained English.

In 1362, the British Parliament began officially using English instead of French. During that same period, the prime literary spokesman of the era, Geoffrey Chaucer, chose to write in English, despite his fluency in French. Today, as a result of France's most recent foreign rule of England, most of the words of learning, refinement and power are French-based, while earlier Scandinavian and Germanic words are used for more common purposes.

The half-million general words in the English vocabulary are about evenly divided between these two sources but thanks to world trade, we now have commonplace words in our vocabularies from all over the world. *Sugar* is Arabic, *chess* is Persian, *cherub* is Hebrew, *mammoth* is Russian, *robot* is Czech, *bizarre* is Basque, *shampoo* is Hindi, *ketchup* is Malay, *hurricane* is from the Caribbean (but *typhoon* is Chinese) and *kangaroo* (you might have guessed this one) is Aboriginal Australian.

Given our motley background, it was inevitable that, over time, a new American dialect would develop. It was codified and formalized thanks largely to the efforts of Samuel Webster who, by writing his <u>American Dictionary of the English Language</u> in 1828, set down once and for all what it was that those upstart provincials were saying.

Webster's dictionary set the American practice of writing *-er* or *-re* (e.g., *theater*), *-or* for *-our* (*favor*), *check* for *cheque, connection* for *connexion, jail* for *gaol,* and a few others. Aside from these and the obvious lexical differences between the dialects (e.g., *elevator* for *lift*), the British also generally favor treating collective nouns as plurals (*the audience were*) and actively change nouns to verbs (*to author*). In addition, Americans generally use *will* rather than *shall, have got* for *have* and pronounce the unstressed syllables that Britons often drop, such as *lab'ratory* instead of the British *laborat'ry.* But, all in all, differences between "British Received Pronunciation" and "General American" today are really quite few and dwindling fast thanks to global communications.

Anyone's English today is certainly one of the most flexible and adaptable languages in the world, largely due to its relatively few inflections (form changes), which, in other languages, tend to "lock" forms and not allow variations with a grammar. German, for example, is highly inflected with five forms for the word *man.* Chinese, at the opposite extreme, has only one form. English has four but, unlike other European languages, only inflects nouns, pronouns and verbs, not adjectives (except *this, that, these* and *those*). For example, only in English do we use *tall* to describe both men and women. Other European languages all use inflected forms, such as the Spanish *alta* or *alto,* depending on the gender of the object described.

This lack of inflection and, hence, rigidity has allowed English-speakers to be delightfully imaginative in creating new forms. Now we can *"plan a table"* or *"table a plan", "lift a thumb"* or *"thumb a lift."* In all other languages in our linguistic "family," nouns and verbs can never be interchangeable due to their special grammatical endings.

The real richness in development of the language today, however, lies in the use of **affixes**, Added either to the front ("prefix"), back ("suffix") or middle ("infix"), these are the building blocks of modern English. The word suffix *-er*, for example, can denote the doer of an action *(farmer)*, the instrument *(harvester)*, or the area *(New Yorker)*.

"Composition" lets us join words to create altogether new compound words. *Already* has come to differ from *all ready*. A *gentle man* may or not be a *gentleman*. (The Chinese use composition very freely to create words like *fly machine* for *airplane*, and *electric language* for *telephone*.)

"Back-formations" are intriguing words, created by the mistaken extension of words back to non-existent stems. For example, *to edit* was derived from *editor* by some long-forgotten goof who wrongly assumed that the words are related to each other in the way *actor* is *to act*. Likewise, *to bulldoze, to televise,* and *to commute* are also new words with no true etymology.

"Blends" are also very popular and becoming more so, especially in politics and in pop culture. *Bang* and *smash* become *bash; smoke* and *fog* become *smog,* while a *motor cavalcade* becomes a *motorcade* and a *cable telegram* becomes a *cablegram.* (The Japanese are famous for their fondness of blends, too. *Radio-cassette* was apparently too cumbersome to say so it was shortened to *raji-kase,* while *mass communications* (what they call "the media) became *masu-komi.*)

The Latin alphabet had all the letters of our modern Roman alphabet except *j, k, v, w, y* and *z.* The Romans added *k* to help with abbreviations and *y* and *z* to help transcribe Greek. *W* was added (as you might guess) as a "double *u*" while *j* and *v* were added as consonant variants of *i* and *u.* Today, we use all 26 letters in both uppercase, or capital, and lowercase, or small, letters.

These 26 letters are used to represent the 44 sounds of English with its 12 vowels, 9 diphthongs (vowel combinations) and 23 consonants. These consonants include six "plosives' (*p, b, t, d, k,* and *g*), six "fricatives" (*f, v, th* as in *thin, th* as in *then, s, z, sh* as in *ship, s* as in *pleasure,* and *h*), two "affricatives (*ch* as in *church* and *j*), the nasals (*m, n* and *-ng* as in *young*), the "lateral" *l,* the "retroflex" *r,* and the "semivowels" *y* and *w.* Three of the letters (*q, c,* and *x*) are redundant since they duplicate either *k* or *ks.*

Unlike the sounds of the consonants which are the same wherever English is spoken, the language's five vowels are pronounced differently according to dialect. American English has 13 vowel sounds and four diphthongs (blended vowels). The American vowels include those sounds found in *eat. sit. ate, get, had, not, saw, so, put, you, son, her* and *up.* The diphthongs are the vowel sounds in *I, cow, boy,* and *few.* Again, these sounds are only for the North American dialect and will vary widely in other countries and sometimes in North America itself, depending on what is standard pronunciation in the region.

Critics of the language claim that we have too few letters representing too many sounds--it's bound to make spelling confusing. On the other hand, our consonants and consonant clusters are fairly unambiguous. We don't use diacritical marks above the letters like French, German, Spanish, Russian and other European languages and just about anyone familiar with any Latin or any Romance language can often make a pretty good guess as to the meaning of an unfamiliar word. (Unfortunately, this doesn't do the Asian student a lot of good.)

At least as difficult as spelling for the student is the fact that English is a heavily stressed language which uses stress and emphasis in very meaningful ways. For example, *record* and *permit,* are changed from nouns to verbs just by shifting the stress from the first to second syllable. Consider, too, the different nuances possible by changing emphasis from one word to the next in the sentence, *I walked to the theater.* By emphasizing different words, different questions can be answered with that one sentence: *Who walked to the theater? How did you get to the theater?* and *Where did you walk to?* (Most grammarians now accept the placement of prepositions at the end of sentences as standard.)

Today, largely because of the immense size and influence of America and its impact on world events, American English is the standard outside Britain's immediate sphere of influence (e.g., Europe and former colonies such as Singapore and Hong Kong). In Japan, "the King's English" was preferred for decades until Japan's trade with America skyrocketed and Britain's influence on the world stage faded. Korea and Taiwan got hooked on the American variety as a result of massive trade with the US, military alliances and an on-going love affair with American culture.

But like any dialect anywhere, neither British nor American English is considered any "better" than the other. There is no such thing as "bad" English so long as members of the speaker's group share that speech pattern and don't view it as non-standard. What makes "standard" English desireable to students is that it is the dialect of money and status--the likely goals of your students. But it's important that you make them understand that the world is full of dozens of kinds of English which, as long as the sub-cultures' members agree on usage, are all perfectly OK. *And don't let nobody tell ya no different, nohow!*

# Popular Teaching Methodologies

Once man decided to interact with his foreign fellows, second language learning became essential. The first "world language" (at least in the Western world) was Greek, language of the dominant culture and a convenient medium of communication for the trading nations of the Mediterranean. Formalized learning of other languages, however, began with the Romans around the third century B.C. when they realized that the Greek civilization had much to teach them.

This study of Greek encouraged the Romans to define the workings of their own Latin and by the first century B.C., Latin was being taught regularly throughout the empire, becoming the second world language and serving that function well into the 18th Century as learned men and women of the West used it in their business, culture and religion.

The usual method of learning Latin and indeed other languages up to the last century was <u>grammar translation</u>. This excruciatingly boring process had the students study long lists of grammatical rules and vocabulary of the target language, then spend hours translating passages back and forth from one language to the other.

Very little time was spent in using the language for free communication of student thoughts, a limitation which virtually guaranteed that the student would have tremendous difficulty ever using the target language for anything but more tedious translation. Sadly, "grammar translation" is the method of choice of Asian public schools for the learning of English, encouraging private schools to go to the opposite extreme of almost never stressing instruction in English grammar in their classes. Other methods are considerably more humane.

The <u>natural</u> <u>method</u> developed in Europe in response to the ineffectiveness of grammar-translation. Naturalists believed it should be possible for a student to learn a second language as he had learned his first: by exposure and figuring things out in his own unique way.

They argued that 1) repetition is as important for second-language learners as for first; 2) language learning is an imitative act; 3) the sequence of learning must be sounds, then words, then whole sentences; 4) listening, then speaking should be taught; 5) reading and writing are more advanced skills than speaking and listening; 6) translation shouldn't be necessary and 7) grammar instruction should not be called for since, after all, children are rarely taught or even aware of their mother tongue's grammar.

Unfortunately, users of this method found that the student's first language interfered with learning the second and that the natural method didn't take advantage of the mature student's ability to logically analyze the second language to facilitate learning. Nor was there the same motivation in the second language as existed in the first. The child is essentially mute until he learns his first language. The second language student can already get by quite nicely in his mother tongue and so doesn't have quite the same sense of urgency no matter how driven he may be to speak the target language.

The <u>direct</u> <u>method</u> is probably the most popular method in language instruction today. With it, the student's own language is never used, creating a different world in the classroom in which the target language is the only acceptable mode of communication. As used by the Berlitz schools (probably the method's biggest booster), the teacher presents a story and students memorize entire sentences from it, later answering questions about the story. Grammar and vocabulary are taught incidentally or at the end of the lesson.

One of the best variations on the direct method is that used by the US military which emphasizes teaching of the target language's culture as well as the language itself. Classes are very intensive, taught only by a native speaker who emphasizes colloquial rather than formal speech. The success rate of students is quite high but not many ordinary classes could allow 15-hour-per-week sessions and regular extracurricular sessions with native speakers.

In reaction to earlier emphasis on reading, a type of direct method called the <u>audiolingual method</u> (or <u>ALM</u>) became quite popular in the 1960s and '70s. With the <u>"aural-oral"</u> method, material is first presented in a dialogue in a highly controlled way to minimize student errors. The students then mimic and memorize (<u>"mim-mem"</u>) some of what the teacher has read. Later, drills are used to manipulate the various grammatical structures introduced although little formal analysis of grammar is done. Outside of class, there is regular use of language laboratories where students mimic native speakers' tapes, emphasizing pronunciation.

ALM counted on repetition of material to form habits of speech which would cause learners to use the target language automatically. This was believed to be a much more "natural" approach and one that allowed the second language learner to approximate the same path taken by him when he learned his first language.

Some linguists like the renowned Noam Chomsky, however, believed that adult learners needed to have their intellects engaged for effective language learning. He and his followers offered the "cognitive" approach as an alternative and the battle between "rote" and "meaningful" learning was begun.

In the mid-1960s, the <u>cognitive</u> <u>approach</u> emphasized use of the target language for free communication and freely explained grammar rules to that end. Pronunciation was deemphasized with the reasoning that it was pointless if not impossible to sound like a native speaker. Errors were seen as signs of development and inevitable. Silence was seen as a useful part of internalization of the language and repetition (if not personally meaningful) was considered of limited value.

In 1972, Caleb Gattegno introduced one of the most innovative methods called <u>The</u> <u>Silent</u> <u>Way</u>. With it, the teacher is largely a facilitator and speaks as little as possible, trying constantly to engage the student's mind. Props are frequently used by the teacher using this method, usually a set of small colored rods which she places in different configurations for the student's analysis, modeling the correct utterance only once.

Because students are frequently left to figure such configurations out on their own without a lot of teacher assistance, there is indeed a great deal of silence in the lesson. Proponents of the method, however, believe that, as with other cognitive methods, this is useful silence in which the student's mind is working, or a Gattegno puts it, "throwing the learner on himself." Supposedly, lessons learned this way are more meaningful and consequently more memorable, but some teachers find the lack of repetition and assistance and the rigid presentation of new material somewhat stifling.

One interesting and much-discussed new method is <u>counseling</u> <u>learning</u> developed by Charles Curran and later adopted in linguistics as <u>Community</u> <u>Language</u> <u>Learning</u> (<u>CLL</u>). In this, the class of language students is assembled in a circle with a native speaker facilitator (or "knower") wandering behind them. Anytime one student wishes to talk to another about anything at all, he may do so by addressing the group in the target language. If he can't say what he wants to, he speaks in his native language and the facilitator makes a translation which the student then repeats to the individual addressed.

At the end of a fifteen minute session, a tape recording of it is analyzed by the group. In its final stages, color-coded lights are used to signal non-verbally to the group if an error has been made, if a more suitable expression could be used or if the communication was correct. Unfortunately, time constraints and the scarcity of truly bilingual facilitators make CLL something of a luxury.

Asher's <u>Total</u> <u>Physical</u> <u>Response</u> found great popularity in the late 1970s as it encouraged students to get physically involved in the target language. The teacher restricted his instructions to the target language and told students to move about the classroom, performing various common tasks such as opening the door, erasing the blackboard, giving paper to another student, etc. It was believed (and still is by many) that such movement reinforces the language lesson.

The results with TPR have been impressive. Within thirty minutes of first-time instruction, students of Japanese have been able to correctly respond to the teacher's instruction: *isu kara tatte, kokuban ni anata no namae o kaite* ("stand up and write your name on the blackboard"). And best of all, retention even after one year was excellent.

<u>Suggestology</u> (or <u>suggestopedia</u>) is a faintly mystical method developed in Eastern Europe by Bulgarian psychologist Georgi Lozanov. Lozanov maintains that his method is appropriate not only for language learning but for any subject. Basically, it seeks to overcome negative "suggestions" or inhibitions which block learning. Such fears include feelings of incompetence, fear of making mistakes and apprehension toward the unfamiliar.

To deal with this, suggestology makes liberal use of mood creation. Music is frequently played to relax students and the teacher assumes the role of almost a therapist, exceedingly trustworthy and gentle. Classrooms ideally resemble living rooms wherein the student's comfort is of paramount importance so as to open the avenues of learning.

Students are given new names in the target culture and encouraged to assume a new identity in the classroom. Homework is minimal but students are asked to come to class somewhat familiar with the many dialogues presented each lesson. These dialogues are initially read by the teacher with background mood music and finally in concert by the students. Conversation is encouraged with extensive correction coming only much later in the course.

Critics say suggestology students lack accurate grammar but there's no denying that they are generally more fluent by virtue of their lessened inhibitions. Because they are usually more willing to communicate, they have been shown to acquire proficiency at a faster rate than students taught by more traditional methods.

Such affective (dare we call them "touchy-feely?") methods as suggestology come from a growing concern in linguistic circles for personality variables in second language learning. Alexander Guiora suggests that there is such a thing as a "language ego" which, in essence, is the persona the student adopts in the language classroom. Guiora says that ego and self-identity are inseparable parts of learning a language because communication is such a fundamentally human activity.

He makes a good point in stating that children learn their first language at a time when their egos are growing and flexible. The new language poses no "threat" to their self-esteem so the child can freely practice the language (and more importantly, make mistakes) without feeling stupid or inept. Puberty apparently defines the ego and establishes defense mechanisms which discourage the adult language learner from taking chances and "acting like a fool" to practice the language.

Along these same lines, Guiora conducted a test among students of Thai. By administering small amounts of alcohol, he found that a student's pronunciation improves markedly once inhibitions are somewhat lessened, even by artificial means. But, although it appears that students really would speak better with a pre-class cocktail, there hasn't been any evidence that other aspects of language except pronunciation improve with booze. Still, in my view, inhibition and fear of errors are primary causes of the dismal record Oriental students have with English.

This wealth of methods alternately emphasizing or prohibiting the mother tongue, grammar study and even errors in the classroom demonstrates just how imprecise the art of language instruction is. Even academics who have built their tenure on the study of the effectiveness of such methodologies will occasionally confess to not knowing what works best. Everyone does agree, however that the student's sincere desire to learn and the teacher's enthusiasm are probably key.

Students usually don't enjoy saying what is incomprehensible to them but they do enjoy sharing a true thought in a foreign language. They loathe what they see as meaningless tasks and dislike mechanical repetitions. Most of all, language students don't learn unless they want to. Motivation and personal involvement are the bedrock upon which success in a foreign language rests.

# Teaching English as a Foreign Language

The demand for teachers of English around the world has certainly never been greater than it is right now. With almost every ex-Communist country trying to plug itself into the global market, more people than ever are keen to learn the World Language. Still, to teach English, it's really not enough just to be a native speaker. Without training or experience, your classroom efforts may not be worth the students' time or tuition. Although a serious look at the *Quick Guide to English Grammar* in this book's Appendix will prepare you somewhat, nothing beats a practice stint in the classroom.

One of the best and easiest (not to mention kindest) ways you can get some practice at the blackboard is to volunteer for some adult English teaching to refugees. Almost every large city has its pocket of immigrants who are desperate to learn some of their new home's language. The community tries to help, usually with free classes, but with current budget cuts, classes are few and overcrowded.

You can help your new neighbors and yourself by volunteering to your county's Board of Education. As a volunteer, no experience is required and, depending on what refugee groups are in your city, you can request an Asian class (probably mostly Vietnamese, Chinese, Laotian or Cambodian). It's a great way to do well by doing good and you'll never have more appreciative students!

Even those of us who have a few years of experience under our belts aren't quite sure half the time what to call what we do. You can call it TEFL, TESL, TESP, TESOL or TENES depending on the type of English you teach and your desire to confuse yourself and those around you. In fact, each variant is slightly different from the others, usually depending on the particular needs of the student being taught.

Although teaching materials and methods may vary a bit depending on the nomenclature, I prefer to use "TEFL" in a more-or-less generic sense to describe teaching English to non-native speakers. This is because, in every other case as well, English is, for the student, a foreign language.

TEFL correctly refers only to Teaching English as a Foreign Language, that is, in an environment such as Asia where English is not a standard medium of communication. Students in such a situation have the luxury of not having to depend on their grasp of English for survival in a foreign country so their commitment to learning it is often less than that of ESL students.

TESL means Teaching English as a Second Language and it describes teaching English to someone such as an immigrant to America who will be using the language on a regular basis for everyday life. It also describes the teaching of English in places like the Philippines where native languages like Tagalog are primary but English is a nationally-known second language.

TESP is an up-and-coming area of instruction wherein instructors teach English for Special Purposes. This practice has developed to meet the needs of people like engineers who don't really have the time to learn *"this is a pen"* but have a great yearning to learn such utterances as *"this is a variable transducer."* Schools offering ESP courses all over the world are in great need of professional people with specialized knowledge willing and able to teach their jargon to eager English students. Because of their export activities, Asian countries have a great need for ESP teachers familiar with business, engineering, computers and other knowledge-based professions.

TESOL is best known as the name of the largest professional organization for ESL/EFL teachers. But it also stands simply for *Teachers of English to Speakers of Other Languages*, a nice catchall description which rivals only TENES or Teachers of English to Non-English Speakers for top honors in blandness. The rule of thumb for the field is, if you're teaching overseas, it's probably TEFL and if you're teaching domestically, it's probably TESL.

Unfortunately, despite the huge demand for EFL instructors worldwide, there has been little agreement as to what methods or tools work best. The primary reason for this (aside from the relative youth of the field) is that every student is as different as every teacher and no one knows what combination, with materials used as catalyst, is most effective.

Generally speaking, lessons are "sequenced" from easy to difficult. There are certain fundamental elements of the language (such as the *be* verb) which must be firmly in place before the student can progress to more sophisticated forms. The *Quick Guide to English Grammar* in the Appendix is sequenced in a more-or-less appropriate manner for students.

More and more, however, ESL/EFL teachers are moving away from the traditional grammar sequencing syllabus and toward what's called the "notional-functional syllabus." This means that while there remains sequencing of grammatical forms based on degree of difficulty, the teacher doesn't just teach, for example, everything the student has never wanted to know about gerunds. Instead, he will teach in a typical lesson everything the student might need to know to order in a restaurant.

Frequently, the lesson will loosely revolve around a particular grammar point appropriate to the "function" being presented (for example, use of *I'll have*"), but mostly it's an effort to teach students discrete chunks of survival-type English, immediately usable in their daily lives. As you'd imagine, this is especially popular and useful for people living in the country of the target language.

In EFL, it is typical to introduce a lesson and grammatical structure with a _dialogue_, usually between two speakers. The teacher typically _models_ the dialogue for the students, taking first one role, then the other so the students can hear the rhythm and pronunciation of a native speaker. Ideally, the dialogue should include material recently learned by the students as well as one or two new items which will serve as a focus of the lesson. Speakers' lines should be short but very natural. Greetings for the speakers aren't necessary unless they are part of the lesson; they usually tend to slow down the readings.

Many teachers have their students memorize the dialogue although most Asian students probably wouldn't if they were just taking the class as a hobby. Certainly, choral, group and finally individual readings of the dialogue are a good idea as well as personal explanation of the lesson's target structure.

In keeping with today's "_cognitive approach_" to language learning, use of the student's native language isn't usually forbidden but it certainly is discouraged. Still, if the teacher knows the students' language, a lot of time can be saved by presenting a brief explanation in that language rather than having to resort to convoluted and confusing elaborations in the target language.

Probably the single most important thing the language teacher can bear in mind as she stands in front of her class is that it is _not_ her show. The tremendous amount of "_teacher talk_" produced by instructors who feel obliged to "perform" for the students and keep up non-stop patter lest the students start snoozing has been a problem since the Romans told their students how to learn Greek rather than letting them practice it themselves. The good teacher speaks in class only enough to get the students talking in the target language.

One good way to encourage students to take a more active part in the class is to assign small classroom-management tasks to them. Students can call roll, return corrected papers, read announcements, etc. These chores, however minor, can develop a sense of teamwork, the learning of names and, most importantly, that it's the students' class too and they should take an active role in it.

Teachers are fairly evenly divided as to the desirability of assigning names in the target language to students. I prefer to let students select English names from my pre-approved list because the foreign name not only gives them good pronunciation practice but it also allows the student to assume a "safe" role in the classroom. As "Larry," he can afford to make mistakes but as the real "Tanaka-san," he might feel inhibited by his position in his company or by the presence of his class/workmates. A list of useful names stressing typical Asian pronunciation problems is included in the Appendix.

Teachers also must decide whether to use an inductive or deductive approach in presenting new material. If you prefer to teach inductively, you just present material without explanation and expect your students to discern in their own way what was happening in the reading, drill, or whatever. A deductive approach, of course, is just the opposite with rules explained first, then examples given to demonstrate those rules in action.

Many teachers combine the two by administering a dialogue first without explanation of the new structure presented and giving a few examples of what's happening linguistically. This allows the students the opportunity to form some idiosyncratic rules about it, then explain the rule at work as they think it can best be stated. Drill and examples drawn from students' personal experiences then help to reinforce knowledge of it. All in all, though. the deductive approach is favored, simply because both teachers and students generally prefer to know what's going on at the outset of the lesson.

Let's look at the usual steps taken in the teaching of a particular lesson:

* <u>Determining</u> what students need to be taught.
* <u>Finding</u> or creating a realistic dialogue or other reading demonstrating this point.
* <u>Modeling</u> it to the students.
* <u>Reading</u> it as a group, then individually.
* <u>Explaining</u> what is being taught by it by stating the language rules at work.
* <u>Checking</u> for understanding by suggesting different situations where the structure might be used.
* <u>Practicing</u> the structure with drills so it becomes internalized.
* <u>Expanding</u> it into personal and independent communication by having the students describe their own experiences using the new structure.
* <u>Reviewing</u> the structure at a later time to reinforce it and ensure retention.

Corrections of students should be handled delicately. It's generally acknowledged now that mistakes are a natural and probably necessary part of learning a language. It's important not to make the student feel foolish for making them. At the same time, it's equally important not to let the student think his major flub was acceptable English. Many teachers favor "<u>expansions</u>" for this purpose so the student isn't made to feel like a dolt but also gets the message that he misspoke.

Essentially, when the teacher expands on what the student says, he "echoes" back what he said but in the correct form. The student might say, for example, _"I told my friend I going to America"_ and the teacher would reply with something like _"Yes, I_ *remember when I told my friend I was going to Japan."*

Denser students might very well think your expansions are just inane comments, of course, so it's probably a good idea to inform the class of how this corrective practice works so they listen attentively to what you're echoing back to them. For those who still don't get it, you can get the student to correct himself by leading him back to where his language failed by saying, in this case, *"I told my friend I...?"*

Many times, a student will consistently fail to correct a grammatical error despite repeated corrections by the teacher. One reason for this may be that the error has become "fossilized" or fixed in the student's mind, probably because some earlier teacher failed to correct it. Such bad linguistic habits are tough to break but making the student aware that he is unconsciously making the same mistake regularly usually causes him to pay attention to it.

Another type of common error is what results from a learner's "<u>interlanguage</u>." The interlanguage, linguists believe, is an idiosyncratic way of speaking which almost all language learners develop to allow them simple communication. It's not a major problem as long as it is merely a temporary stage in their acquisition of the language. But if, for example, the student consistently drops the final *-s* in third person singular constructions for too long without correction, such errors can become <u>fossilized</u>. The world is full of people who speak a foreign language very comfortably and confidently--and very badly.

In my opinion, if a teacher isn't correcting, she's not doing her job--even if the correction is unwelcome. Asian students aren't bad about accepting corrections (let's not talk about Arabs) but once in a while you'll have a student who's sure he knows it all. Slouching in his chair at the back of the classroom, he's already been to the States where he spent a week in Malibu with his American surfer buddy. Based on this, he's sure his English is entirely adequate. "For sure," he whines, "everybody know what I say meaning. Why I must do boring study?" It's essential that you clean up this garbage, hopefully before it's become so ingrained in his speech that the habit can't be broken--and he's doomed to a lifetime of career-limiting poor English.

On the other hand, it's very important not to interrupt a good flow of target language use with corrections. If the teacher is part of a give-and-take conversation with a student, expansions can correct usage in a fairly unobtrusive way. Students frequently will ask teachers to correct them whenever they make a mistake but it quickly becomes obvious that conversation would be virtually impossible with constant corrections.

A better way to keep the flow going and correct students is to keep a log of individual students' mistakes. Most students have particular areas of grammar in which they are shaky and subtle notes during student speeches, drills and group exercises can quickly identify them for later work.

A student's area of weakness can also be spotted by regular "avoidance" of a particular structure. You may find that a particular student will bend over backwards to avoid using the present perfect (_have + verb_), preferring to always use, say, the simple past tense which many times works perfectly well. Avoidance can be recognized many times by the student opting for a more complex or longer sentence rather than one using a simple, but difficult sound or grammatical construction.

Of course, to recognize errors, you have to have a good grasp of what you're teaching. This may seem like a ludicrous point to be making, but I would suggest that you take a long, hard look at the quality of _your_ English. Use this book as one measure of your English ability--it's targeted at literate, university-graduate native speakers. Obviously, the audience is American but British, Canadian and Australian readers should have no trouble grasping every nuance.

Don't delude yourself if you're non-native. Of course you may understand the gist of everything I'm saying but if there is *any* word or phrase you aren't familiar with, think about your actual command of English. Don't assume that just because, for example, you've lived in the States for 10 years, graduated from an American university and all your American friends say you're English is fine, that you can teach the stuff. Unless absolutely desperate for foreign teachers, only true native speakers are hired for language instruction overseas anywhere in the world.

If in doubt about your English, call the Educational Testing Service at (609)951-1100 and tell them you want to take the International Test of English as a Foreign Language (TOEFL). They'll send you an information bulletin with all the upcoming test sites and dates listed and a registration form. The test is administered monthly and at a cost of about $40, it might be good reassurance that your English is up to the job. A perfect score is 677 and personally, I'd say any score under 600 would mean you might have a hard time finding teaching work.

Vocabulary, of course, is an essential element of language instruction but there can be too much of a good thing. Oriental students tend to have impressive vocabularies thanks to their public school's emphasis on grammar-translation. Unfortunately, like a computer without a program, there's not much they can do with all those words until they learn how to make them work together.

Teachers generally agree nowadays that it's a poor idea to teach vocabulary items in isolation. The words need to be associated with something meaningful in the student's life, if only that lesson's dialogue. The first words you'll want to teach (if the students have forgotten them), of course, are the ones necessary for the class: listen, repeat, say, ask, and answer.

It should also be explained to students early on that there are content-type words (with meaning) and there are function-type words (for grammar, e.g. _the_). The Japanese are especially keen to learn the derivatives of lexical (dictionary) meanings. Teaching _travel, traveler_ and _well-traveled_ shows the student how English affixes work and makes vocabulary-building seem logical. Be careful, however, not to teach so many derivatives that the students become overwhelmed. Three or four derivatives per item is probably as much as they can handle.

An intermediate EFL student should probably have a vocabulary of about 2,000 English words. These should include all numbers (both cardinal and ordinal), dates, addresses, measurements (such as age, weight, height, time, distance and money), common foods, days of the week, months, seasons, clothing, utensils, body parts, furniture, family relationships, colors, shapes and sizes, cities and countries, common animals, common occupations, common activities. Either written or orally, you might want to give a brief test on these items to your class to see who knows what. Many times, students will know incredibly sophisticated words but will have gaping holes in their knowledge of everyday terms.

Idioms and slang (the "spice" of any language) are always popular items of study and, since they are a very real part of our language, should certainly be shared with students. It's very important, however, to explain thoroughly to students at the time these are presented that they are not appropriate for all situations--usually only the most casual. If, thanks to your failure to warn him, the Japanese student someday asks his conservative American client if he wouldn't like to "toss back some brewskies" with him after work, you might have done him a bit of a disservice. On the other hand...

"Register" refers to the speaker's level of formality which may change according to the social environment. It isn't a social or regional dialect but rather a special variety of language used for a specific purpose. A primary way to distinguish a child's use of language from that of an adult is the degree to which she is able to vary styles according to the social situation. Much research on this has shown that even in supposedly egalitarian America, people regularly use register (often unconsciously) to change their speech to fit the situation.

Linguist Martin Joos in his fascinating book, The Five Clocks, refers to five different levels of formality in English, each with different forms of speech: the oratorical or frozen level, the deliberative or formal level, the consultative level, the casual level and the intimate level.

The oratorical style, says Joos, is used mostly in public speaking with carefully chosen wording, somewhat exaggerated intonation and many rhetorical devices. The deliberative style is used when size of the audience makes personal interaction impossible. It is a more informal style than the oratorical but words are also carefully chosen for essentially pure information transmission such as one might find in a large university lecture.

Businessmen and doctors use the consultative style with clients wherein words are still carefully chosen and formality is maintained. Casual style is used among friends where social barriers are few and words are not especially guarded. An intimate style is used among close friends and family members with whom complete honesty can be granted without inhibitions.

In Asia, especially, conversation is king. Students all clamor for it and school officials all promise it to them in the form of a real-live native speaker. Unfortunately, there's a terrific potential for a real waste of time if the teacher spends all of his time trying to get students to engage in free conversation before they're relaxed or prepared enough. Oftentimes, too, the teacher feels compelled to address "significant issues" during the conversation period when, in fact, students often prefer simple but sincere inquiries into their own lives, so long as the teacher isn't intrusive.

Free conversation certainly plays an essential role in language acquisition but too often, such sessions wind up with the teacher doing all the talking, having the "conversation" dominated by a handful of assertive students or (every teacher's worst nightmare) dead silence while the desperate teacher tries to get the students to say something, _anything._

Make sure that you have sufficient rapport with the students and that they have the linguistic tools available before you throw open the doors of conversation. Many times, your students will need a lot of preliminary work before they engage in meaningful conversation.

Rather than opening the class to free conversation, often engaging the students in "role play" serves the same purpose but gives better focus to the proceedings. For example, if the day's lesson has been on the _wh-_ question words (_who, what,_ etc.), students could be paired off and told they are a newspaper reporter and a crime victim or a detective and his suspect. Since so many English students in Asia are businessmen, role plays about meeting a foreign businessperson are especially popular and useful, almost qualifying as ESP (English for Special Purposes). Of course, figuring out what a class of unresponsive students wants or needs from you sometimes calls for an altogether different kind of ESP...

Breaking the class up into small groups is an excellent way to multiply the amount of time each student speaks in class. In my view, small groups should be formed as much as possible and whenever the students can be given something substantive to work on for at least 10 minutes.

There are conflicting views in teaching about how to structure small groups. Some teachers like to cluster all the dominant students in a single group to allow the more reticent ones to speak freely whereas other teachers believe more articulate students act as catalysts for quieter students and so they should be mingled.

In the homogeneous classes found overseas, the teacher must be very strict about not allowing the native language to be spoken. The students probably will feel foolish speaking broken English to each other when their natural language is so accessible but they will comply if they know you're serious about it. Some teachers set up a "fine" system whereby students must contribute, for example, fifty cents to a "party kitty" each time they slip up and use their native language.

<u>Drills</u> are an important part of every language class, much as students (and some teachers) may loathe them. They're still the most effective means we have to demonstrate how a grammatical structure functions and changes, to reinforce it in the mind of the student, and to test the student's comprehension of it.

The well-respected EFL/ESL academic, Wilga Rivers, suggests that teachers remember the following "rules of drill:"

* Drills are for teaching not testing.
* Give plenty of practice in each element before moving to the next.
* Stick to one specific structural element (don't try to teach more than one thing per drill).
* The feature you're drilling should have been part of an earlier activity (e.g., a dialogue).
* Keep changes from one item to the next small.
* Keep the items short.

* Each item should be a natural, realistic utterance.

* The teacher's cue should ideally prompt only one proper response.

* Keep vocabulary simple.

* Drill orally and only in the target language.

* Vary the types of drill.

* Arrange for students to use drill material in meaningful communication immediately after the drill is completed.

The most common "manipulative drills" are repetition, substitution (either single- or multiple-slot), transformation, completion, expansion, paraphrasing and integrative. Among "meaningful drills we have restatements and rejoinders, and question and answer.

Repetition is simply having students echo back exactly what the teacher says, usually first as a group (choral), then smaller groups (e.g., first males, then females; right side of class, then left side of class) and finally individuals, either volunteers or "victims."

Single-slot substitution drills have the students given a sentence or question and cue word. They must then insert the cue word in the same place in the sentence. For example: "_I go to the store every day. Week._" = "_I go to the store every week._"

Multiple-slot substitution drills simply allow the student to place the new word anywhere in the original sentence where it would be correct. For example: "_I go to the park every week. He._" = "_He goes to the park every week._" Then "_movies_" = "_He goes to the movies every week._"

Transformation drills have the student change the form of the sentence or question. For example, "_I go to the store every week._" = "_Do you go to the store every week?_" This works especially well in "chains" where one student will transform a structure and direct it to another student who then continues with another; e.g., *"Now ask Tomoko."* It's a good way to help minimize "teacher talk."

Completion drills can only be used with certain structural types, such as tag questions. The student merely adds to what the teacher says; e.g., *"He went to the store today."* = *"He went to the store today, didn't he?"*

Expansion drills are very common to help students digest complex sentences when they can't remember the whole thing in a single mental gulp. For example, if the teacher for some odd reason wants the students to say, *"I thought I saw a purple cow but, after careful consideration, I decided I must have been mistaken,"* he would probably have to "build" them to it by starting with, *"I thought I saw"* (they repeat), *"I thought I saw a purple cow"* (repeat), until they have retained the full "udderance" (sorry, just couldn't resist).

Paraphrasing drills can be tricky because they require the student to create a new form. But with sharp intermediate or advanced students who have thoroughly studied what is being drilled, they can be very effective. For example, if you've been explaining how verbs can be made into nouns by adding *-ed*, you might instruct them to paraphrase *"the decorator put carpet on the floor."* = *"The decorator carpeted the floor."*

In teaching <u>affixes</u> (both <u>prefixes</u> and <u>suffixes</u>), paraphrasing can elicit the desired structure. If, for example, you've been teaching *un-*, you might say, *"If the door is locked and you want to get out, you would tell me to..."* = *"Unlock the door, please."*

Integrative drills are very useful to get students to speak more efficiently since it encourages the compounding of phrases. For example, *"I went to the store. He went to the store."* = *"I went to the store and he did too."*

Meaningful drills are those which ask the student to give personal meaning to the response. Restatement drills have the student rephrase a question, often readdressing it in "chain" fashion to another student. For example: *"Bill, ask Sally what she did yesterday"* = *"Sally, what did you do yesterday." "I went to the library. Elliot, what did you do yesterday?"* and so forth around the room.

Rejoinder drills require a fairly high level of proficiency but are excellent practice for real communication. They require the student to listen critically to what the teacher is saying and actually correct a misperception. For example, if the teacher says *"Karen, what countries border Korea besides Russia and Taiwan?"* the student should say something like *"Korea doesn't border Russia or Taiwan."* A simple version of this has the student reply to the teacher with some personal information: e.g., *"I don't smoke."* = *"You don't smoke and neither do I."*

Many people don't regard question and answer as a drill at all, but it could be considered one if the student incorporates the target vocabulary into his response. *"What's your hobby?"* = *"My hobby is playing golf."* It would probably not be a true drill if the student had simply replied, *"I like to play golf."*

In drilling, it's important not to "<u>telegraph</u>" your selected "victim" before stating the problem. If students know they won't be called on, many of them won't bother trying to work the exercise. It's best to state the drill problem, wait a few seconds for *all* the students to think about it and reach an answer, then select a student to respond.

In selecting students, teachers need to be aware of <u>favoritism,</u> often caused by a reluctance to embarrass students whom they think might not know the answer. A study of this showed that teachers indeed don't distribute turns evenly but instead rely on either the brighter students, those who for some reason "look ready" or worse, where the students are sitting in the classroom.

A more equitable system might be to put student names on index cards and just work your way through the stack. To effectively match bright or slow students with the challenging and easier questions, respectively, you could remove student names from the stack of cards after they had answered correctly and then choose from among the remaining students according to the question's difficulty. The problem with this, of course, is that the students who have already answered will know they won't be called on and might not do the drill. It's always best to keep 'em guessing!

Group work is especially good for managing a large class but should also be used liberally in any class since it reduces "teacher talk." Some Japanese students may think this is an unusual way to conduct a class since, in their minds, they came to work with a glamorous foreigner not listen to other students speak broken English.

If you hear such a comment, a good response is that the class is for speaking, not hearing practice and is designed to improve their own personal fluency. It's largely irrelevant whether the hearer of the speaker's efforts is a native or non-native English speaker.

In Asia, your class may be the students' first experience with group work since probably all their other instruction used the lecture format. Therefore, it's probably a good idea to spend part of the first class period explaining the desirability of working in groups and how it will allow each student to spend more time speaking English as students act alternately as student and teacher. Students will also need assurance that the teacher will always be close at hand to answer questions and correct major mistakes as she circles throughout the classroom.

Students should be divided into groups of three to six, depending on the total class size so that you have probably no more than about eight groups. For large classes, a leader should be elected in each group, perhaps after the students have had a chance to evaluate each other's English proficiency by having everyone introduce himself in English.

The leader might then gather members' names, addresses and telephone numbers which are submitted to the teacher. It's always a good idea to have some means of contacting your students in case of emergency and tasking group leaders with calling their group's members saves a lot of phone time. Of course, if you sense any reluctance from students to give out their phone numbers, don't press it.

<u>Speeches</u> and <u>debates</u> are challenging and very useful for the Asian student if only to help them overcome their extreme reluctance to speak publicly. Assigning prepared speeches allows the student sufficient time to feel confident about what he has written but <u>impromptu speeches</u> most closely approximate using English for communication. Subjects should be kept simple and innocuous at first, gradually becoming more controversial and complex as students improve their English and feel more at ease with each other.

Traditional debates have three students on a side giving the <u>presentation, rebuttal</u> and <u>summation,</u> respectively. Judges can be recruited from students unable to debate because of absences in their teams with the teacher reserving veto power in case of favoritism. Good debates can be quite lively and generate a lot of excitement, especially if an elimination system is used where the "finals" pit the two best teams against each other for a stimulating topic. You'll be surprised to see your worst wallflowers turn into real tigers to defend their opinions!

One final word about what may be the most important aspect of your classroom performance: appearance and manners. Asians are very "looks" oriented and tend to think in grossly stereotypical terms: a nicely dressed person is smart, friendly and kind; a person wearing blue jeans is either poor or possibly dangerous. You should be aware that our American insensitivity to dress is quite unique in the world. Especially in conservative Asia, you are what you wear.

Bring a set of nice clothes with you. Coat and tie is sometimes required in Japan and Korea, rarely in tropical Taiwan. Keep your look clean-cut; men with earrings, long-hair, jeans or T-shirts may be courting trouble in the classroom. Women should avoid pants unless they are loose-fitting. Facial hair? Cut it off! You should know that Asians think *any* facial fuzziness looks grubby. Finally, never get angry or threatening with Asians. Even if it feels phony, keep smiling. As anywhere, there's no surer way of getting on with your career in the Orient than by getting on with people.

# Teaching English
# in Japan

English instruction is a huge preoccupation among the Japanese people. Although English is not a required subject in high school, the fact that it is an important part of the dreaded college-entrance exams encourages students to take it the whole time they attend junior and high school. With close to 100% of Japanese graduating from high school, it's probably safe to say that over 90% of adult Japanese have studied the language for six or more years.

The 1/3 of high school graduates who continue on to college typically take the subject for an additional four years so the majority of people whom the average foreigner in Japan encounters (college graduates) have studied English for a good ten years. One conversation with such a person, however, will likely convince you that it was not time well spent.

What many unfortunate Japanese have for their years of English study is what might be called, "inarticulate literacy." Many who've studied the language can read it exceptionally well but precious few can carry on an intelligible conversation with a native speaker. Fortunately, this means plenty of opportunity for English teachers who, the Japanese hope, can unlock the door to English for them.

Education has always been of tremendous importance in the pragmatic Japanese society but, with the Meiji Restoration of 120 years ago, Japan moved its educational efforts into high gear in a desperate attempt to catch up technologically with the rest of the world. Largely because of the country's desire to learn as much as possible about foreign technology through printed matter, a brutally strict form of grammar-translation was adopted for the learning of English.

With this method, the Japanese condemned themselves to almost never being able to converse with an English speaker but soon were able to read almost anything he might write. For the insular Japanese of the time, however, this suited them just fine.

After WWII, however, suddenly there appeared real, live English-speakers by the thousands, right there in the homeland. Suddenly, the focus of English instruction needed to shift from written to spoken but change is excruciatingly slow in Japan.

Nevertheless, with the conquest of their country by an English-speaking army and the perceived economic dominance of the world by that victor, the Japanese were quick to see the value of learning the language believing whole-heartedly that "if you can't beat 'em, join 'em til you can." After having been almost banned during the war, English has grown in popularity today to such an extent that even those who could have no possible use for it study eagerly just to conform to the national mania.

Excessive as it may be, the Japanese love of English (or should we say, the love of the _learning_ of English?) translates into lots of jobs for native English speakers wishing to spend time in the country. And since most of the Japanese students have had years of grammar and vocabulary instruction, schools believe that all the students really need is "conversation," however a particular school happens to interpret that rather vague instructional goal.

Most small schools think conversation teachers don't really need credentials since, popular thinking goes, anyone can teach "conversation" in their native language. Teaching experience and credentials frequently aren't given as much favor in hiring in

Japan as they might be back home and perhaps because of this, there are relatively few teachers with any sort of formal teacher training although many big schools in the 90s are expecting experience in their new hires.

Largely for this reason and the fact that Japanese employers are reluctant to hire anyone sight unseen, few positions are filled from outside the country. Although it is possible to obtain sponsorship as a teacher before actually going to Japan for interviews, it is becoming more difficult as more prospective teachers are willing to go to Japan with only a tourist visa, find a sponsoring employer and then change to a working visa.

Being in Japan tells an employer some important information about you: that you are certainly serious about coming to the country, that you are probably almost over your homesickness and so will probably be fairly stable, that you probably have successfully dealt with other Japanese organizations and that he won't have to pay your airfare over.

To avoid possible problems in these areas, the employer will often hire a less-qualified person locally even though a more-qualified person overseas has indicated absolute willingness to come over.

About the only way to get hired without a personal interview is to be recommended by a person (usually Japanese) whose judgment the employer trusts. Employers certainly would rather not have to interview applicants since frequently the interviewer knows nothing about teaching English and may not even speak it well himself.

Thus, endorsement by a trustworthy Japanese can sometimes do the trick--if not resulting in actual hiring before the interview then at least turning the interview into more of a confirmation. (For more specific information on sponsorship and general hiring practices, please consult my general guidebook, JOBS IN JAPAN, also available from The Global Press.)

In interviewing, common sense should dictate behavior and dress. Dress well and conservatively and make sure all relevant documents (resume, copies of diplomas, recommendations, photos) are in order. Be prepared to answer rather vague questions to test your sincerity such as why you came to Japan, what you think about it, how you think Japan can best "internationalize." The successful interview will result in a contract for usually one year, possibly longer if incentives (such as return airfare) are included.

It is useful to have as your personal sponsor someone not associated with your employment. Every foreigner must have his stay in Japan guaranteed by an individual (it could be another _gaijin_ if they've been there long enough) and most teachers simply let the employing school president act as theirs.

Should there be some dispute about the contract you've signed with the school, however, it could be easier to extricate yourself from it if you have a totally separate person vouching for your character. Having an outside sponsor does give a bit more leverage in settling disputes with or quitting an employer.

Contracts in Japan with foreigners are generally unenforceable insofar as your ultimate out is simply to leave the country. (Don't worry, no one's ever been extradited back to Japan to face charges of classroom desertion.) The Japanese don't really like to rely on contracts either because they're never quite sure what they'll have you doing. They'd prefer to have the flexibility to ask you to do a variety of things and don't want to be limited to what is enumerated in the contract. Part-time instructors (those not given sponsorship by that school) are considered _jigyoosha_ or self-employed (contract) workers, and sometimes aren't even asked to sign contracts.

Many people do indeed ignore contracts and get along fine with their employer (who often sees it as a governmental formality anyway). There is some danger, however, in breaking contract if you want to stay in the country. Anytime a *gaijin* changes employers, Immigration requires a letter of release from the former employer stating the conditions under which the foreigner left his company. (Spouses of Japanese citizens are exempt from this reporting requirement.) It's always best to be cooperative and leave an employer on terms favorable enough to get a positive Immigration letter which will allow you to change to another school.

Japan has always had a sort of love-hate relationship with the West, especially America. On the one hand, Americans are admired for their straight-forwardness, independence, determination, optimism and vigor. On the other, Westerners in general are seen as willful, selfish, argumentative, and somewhat disruptive of the common good. Lately, of course, in light of America's relative decline economically, we're seen merely as whiners, unwilling to get our act together in terms of education and hard-work and blaming everyone but ourselves for our woes.

When Japanese return home after living abroad, one study has shown that the society at large frequently expresses concern that the returnee will be independent rather than dependent, self-reliant rather than group-cooperative, innovative rather than conforming, and responsive only to rational-legal authority rather than personal (group) authority. In short, a misfit.

For the Westerner trying to prove himself in Japan, this approval of conformity and dependence can be confusing and lead to inappropriate behavior, especially in aggressively proposing innovative ideas which the Japanese prefer to leave to senior employees. New workers (teachers or otherwise) are usually discouraged from taking an active administrative role. They are expected instead to learn how things are done traditionally, who holds power and how to avoid offending those individuals.

This, of course, can be very frustrating for the imaginative and dynamic instructor. Still, the sad truth is that schools are great believers in the expression "if it ain't broke, don't fix it." And, unfortunately, a school can be just barely surviving and still not be considered "broke" by its administrators.

Even if a new proposal is accepted, it will frequently fail because the proper channels weren't followed to ensure support among those whose participation is necessary. The Japanese will often pay "lip service" to innovation just to be agreeable but then totally neglect to follow through for successful implementation if the proper "ground work" hasn't been done.

Sociologist Chie Nakane has stated that personal loyalty is everything in Japan. Employees are expected to give undying loyalty to a single powerful figure and, for their support, they are rewarded by him. Needless to say, "office politics" run rampant in Japanese society, even, to an extent, among foreigners who are in most ways regarded as transient and ultimately expendable guest workers existing more or less outside the office sphere.

What this means for the foreigner seeking to teach in Japan is that the work environment there is an alien one and one which, after a few months of politicizing, she may not want to be actively involved in. Fortunately, the Japanese don't consider us *gaijin* as regular staff people anyway so we are largely relieved of the kind of backstage intrigues the Japanese employees are regularly embroiled in.

By far the largest number of jobs available to native English speakers involve teaching adults, usually businessmen (or, as the Japanese call them, *sarariman*). Schools offer classes in their facility or, more commonly, teachers are sent to the client company's facility to teach employees there. These "in-company" classes with enrollments of between five and fifteen are generally held after the workday, making teaching hours between 5 and 9 p.m. Monday through Friday especially valuable.

Student, client and teacher expectations can vary dramatically with the client's goals sometimes seeming vague if not nonexistent. In one survey, for example, instructors listed their teaching goals as "activation" of past learning (i.e., helping the students recall and use what they'd learned years before in school), "unlearning" incorrect "fossilized" forms of "Japanese English," and "exposure to foreigners and their cultures."

On the other hand, companies listed their goals for employees learning English as being to increase the pool of employees who could use English if the need arose. Another frequently mentioned reason was to "internationalize" (although there has never been consensus on what the term means).

Many companies acknowledge that their employees are frightened of foreigners and simply would like them to learn to interact with _gaijin_ without trembling with terror (I've seen it happen!). Of course, some companies with overseas operations have very real specific English needs for their employees bound for foreign assignments.

Certainly one major expectation of client companies and schools is the development of rapport between teachers and their students. Because exposure to foreigners is a major justification for the classes, it is advisable and sometimes incumbent upon teachers to socialize with their students after class, usually at a local bar or restaurant, where the teacher can be seen to be "just a regular person."

Frequently, the students' company will also invite the teacher to a weekend "retreat" at a company facility for drinking, singing and general merriment. Again, acceptance of the invitation will be strongly urged, probably by your boss who might point out (quite rightly) that it will be a lot of fun. Contrary to what many foreigners think proper behavior would be as a respected *sensei*, Japanese do not expect or appreciate stuffiness or stand-offish behavior from their teacher.

It is sometimes difficult for in-company teachers to plan lessons since attendance is sporadic. Employees work long, irregular hours and English classes are usually considered fairly low priority commitments, appropriate only when more immediate problems aren't pressing. When students do come, they are likely to be tired from the day's grind.

For this reason, it is usually best not to engage them in strenuous activity or assign much homework since they are probably volunteer students and wouldn't stand for more hard work after their regular work day. Pair and small-group work together with exercises allowing the student to use his own work-related knowledge are probably best for this sort of class.

Although such jobs are relatively few, it is possible to work directly for a Japanese company and not a school. One study conducted by the Sanno Institute of Business Administration found that 75% of all foreign employees worked for manufacturing companies. Of all employees, 42% were in public relations or language resources (translation, copywriting, proof-reading, etc.) and 24% were language teachers.

Pay is comparable to a good private school but as a regular employee, the teacher is allowed full benefits which, in a Japanese company, can be considerable: health benefits, bonuses, housing allowances, sometimes even retirement plans and guaranteed employment. For these additional benefits, however, the teacher must work long hours and demonstrate the kind of unwavering loyalty and devotion to the company that is typical of regular employees.

Because the positions are relatively few in number (most companies just don't have the need for a full-time English person) and the involvement in the Japanese work-ethic is rather daunting, first-time or visiting instructors probably shouldn't consider these positions. Too often, they place the foreigner squarely in the middle of the aforementioned maze of office politics, without even having the language skills to deal with it. But if you get such an offer, before you sign on the dotted line, be sure you've examined closely your feelings about singing the company anthem every morning at 8.

Classes in language schools proper (where students come to the schools' facilities for instruction) range in size from a handful of students to sometimes 50 or more. Many of the students will be college-age, either preparing for the difficult college-entrance examinations or seeking to graduate from their college. Other students will be housewives with little real need for English other than to impress their girl friends and feel that they're doing something useful after they've gotten their toddlers off to school.

As private enterprises started by entrepreneurs, they are unregulated and they can teach whatever they like in whatever way they choose. Consequently, no two schools are alike although many use the same texts and other materials. Although most schools are run by legitimate educators, a few are owned and operated by fast-buck artists who will take anyone with tuition to spend and pay teachers as little as possible and then only when pressured to.

To discourage student disenrollment, there is usually a hefty entrance fee charged upon enrollment in addition to monthly tuition. Some schools advance students through a program of instruction; others offer open-ended classes divided by vague levels of proficiency: beginner, intermediate and advanced.

Teachers at such schools are usually recruited either by departing teachers or through advertisements in local English newspapers, especially the Monday edition of *The Japan Times.* Teachers are expected to be, above all, personable and kind, the type of person the student will want to be with even if progress is slow. Pay ranges from about 2,500 to 5,000 yen per hour with remuneration sometimes taking the form of reduced rent in company housing, furniture, telephone, etc. Fringe benefits, "guaranteed employment," retirement plans and medical plans are very rare (although national health insurance can usually be obtained for this last need).

Duties are vague so you're advised to be sure to find out what, if anything, is expected of you in addition to teaching. Extra, unpaid responsibilities are not unusual and should be clarified before any contract is signed.

Many schools will give their teachers a guaranteed number of teaching hours for a set monthly salary with additional hours (which frequently can't be declined) being compensated at an additional rate. Better schools will keep enrollment high and teachers busy. Some smaller schools might allow enrollment to dwindle to where classes will be canceled. At this point, the teacher may be expected to help with recruitment by encouraging current students to continue their studies.

The earliest classes are special before-work sessions where salarymen try to squeeze in a little English before their work day begins. These are fairly rare and the teacher will usually be paid a premium for having to endure rush-hour trains and be at the school by, perhaps, 7:30 a.m.

Later in the morning, after the children are sent off to school, housewife classes are held until about 3 p.m. when after-school children might have their classes. Young children (8-12 years) usually come first, followed by junior high and high school students in the early evening. Adult classes with work-weary businessmen may be held until 9 or 10 p.m.

The average full-time work load of a teacher is about 20 hours per week although many more hours can be taught without too much difficulty if classes don't call for extensive traveling from one location to another. The money can be quite good but opportunities for advancement are few and job security is minimal. To balance this, however, there is always an abundance of jobs elsewhere even though your particular little school might not always be able to give you a class. Teaching English at private schools in Japan frequently is a sort of nomadic existence.

It is theoretically possible to work and support yourself legally just by teaching private lessons on your own. Of course, you do need a Japanese citizen to act as sponsor and you might have to prove to Immigration that you have sufficient savings so that if you aren't able to attract enough students after all, you can still keep yourself from becoming a bagperson. Given that, however, it is remarkably easy to organize private classes by distributing a few well-placed flyers near your local train station and getting out the word that your English is for hire.

To be able to actually support yourself with private classes only, though, you probably would need about a year to develop the necessary connections. Most teachers use private lessons as a means of augmenting their regular paycheck from their sponsor.

All that private classes really call for are textbooks or class reading materials, a blackboard and a space large enough for five to eight students. As with "real" schools, the teacher collects an enrollment fee (usually equal to one month's tuition) from each new student and each month, collects tuition, ordinarily about 2,000 yen per hour per student. Much-sought-after private classes with wealthy businessmen and professionals (usually held at coffee shops) can often pay 10,000 yen an hour and more for simple conversation. Connections provide these gems.

Although there's no denying that students are exceptionally diligent in Japan, one sometimes gets the feeling that education, as measured by ability to actually utilize what is learned, is not so important to school officials as the appearance of hard study and the memorization of voluminous quantities of data. This would certainly seem to be the case in public schools and college-level English instruction.

Japanese scholars are granted tenure as soon as they are hired by a university and it is well-known in academic circles that the scholar's job is research and publication, not instruction. In fact, the teacher who spends too much time working with students is sometimes chastised for being derelict in his scholastic duties. Evaluation is almost non-existent so the college instructor's concern for quality education is low.

Teaching is largely seen as a nuisance and one to be dispensed with as quickly as possible. Students, of course, are aware of this apathy and reflect it with large-scale absenteeism. Says one foreign college English instructor, "Neither teachers nor students, with few exceptions, expect much of themselves or each other." Not surprisingly, since graduation from university is virtually automatic (once the student is accepted based on his performance on the exceedingly difficult entrance exam), it's possible for students to go whole semesters without stepping foot on campus.

So, although university pay (between four and six million yen annually) and work schedules (sometimes as few as 90 days on campus per year) are good, there is great frustration and poor morale in store for the serious teacher. But largely because the positions are so "cushy," competition for them is severe, almost requiring a personal introduction by someone very well-connected to the hiring institution.

Again, however, due to the demoralizing atmosphere of most college English departments and the competition for the few positions, short-term teachers are not advised to apply for them. Good pay, much more fun and greater professional challenge can easily be found elsewhere, usually in the private sector.

Life for the Japanese public school student is not terribly pleasant. Made to wear severe, militaristic uniforms (wholly unflattering and roundly disliked), students are not allowed the same social development common in Western societies. There is no "senior prom" or "homecoming." Dating is not a recognized activity (although rebellious sexual activity is high) and students are expected to repress their budding social needs to prepare for that one crucial event which may well determine the shape of the rest of their lives: the college entrance examination.

English study in such an atmosphere is often bleak, consisting of long lists of vocabulary, English grammar (explained in Japanese by the teacher with the same attention to detail one would expect of a coroner) and frequent, easily-graded multiple-choice exams.

There is little discussion and rarely any vocalization of the language learned. Many students graduate from their English classes totally unfamiliar with the English sound system and, although they may actually "know" English, will regard the foreigner trying to ask directions of him in that language much as they might look at a Martian, grunting and squeaking his plea for interplanetary directions.

In the nationally uniform Japanese school system, there exist virtually no other foreign languages but English. Some believe English in Japan serves a purpose much like Latin's in Western cultures in the last century: a good intellectual exercise, not really intended for actual use. One particularly cynical foreign high school teacher recently termed high school English instruction "an elaborate, intense rite of passage in which the more ambitious of the young people in this country demonstrate their capacity for drudgery and self-denial to the powers-that-be."

To overcome this provincialism, the Japanese government launched an ambitious program in 1987 whereby young native-English speakers are sent into the hinterlands. The Japan Exchange and Teaching Program (JET) offers two types of work: Assistant English Teacher (AET) and Coordinator for International Relations (CIR).

Both CIRs and AETs are usually under 35, are university graduates and have some plausible interest in Japan (other than the fairly attractive salaries). CIRs are also often expected to speak some Japanese since they come in regular contact with members of their local community, helping them organize events, cultural exchanges as well as promoting international trade and tourism.

AETs usually back up the high school students' regular English teacher, serving as a "live specimen" of *Homo Anglicus*. As such, the AET has very little authority in the classroom and is often at odds with the Japanese teacher. Usually the AET wants to teach the kids "real" English while the main teacher just wants to get them through their upcoming entrance exam. Unfortunately, in most cases, the Japanese teacher is right in devoting the class time to "grammar-translation." Everyone knows it's a crashing bore but until the college entrance exams are changed, it's the best way to get them into the university of their choice.

One-year contracts for JETs begin August 1 and can be renewed. Although free-lance work is unlikely due to a fairly full schedule and an often remote location, the annual pay of 3.6 million yen is good compensation. All in all, the JET program is a good chance to work outside the major cities and get to know the "real" Japan (if such a thing exists anymore!) See the relevant section in my <u>JOBS</u> <u>IN</u> <u>JAPAN</u> and contact your Japanese embassy for further details.

Partly in response to the national cry for "internationalization," more and more parents are seeking to give their wee ones a leg-up in Japan's educational rat race by having them begin their English studies at an early age. Frequently, such parents are returning from an overseas assignment where the child very quickly picked up English from friends and they seek to have him retain and develop what he's learned.

Other parents simply realize that it's best to start language habits at an early age. Ordinarily, by the time most students begin studying English in junior high school, the language has become "externalized" and can never be learned in a "natural" fashion again.

Many children's classes are organized on a casual basis by enterprising teachers in their own neighborhood. Pay is usually per child per hour and should exceed in total what the teacher is accustomed to receiving at her regular teaching job.

Six to ten students is probably an ideal size but children's classes at schools can sometimes contain as many as 30, especially in after-school *juku* ("cram schools") where students come to augment their school studies. When that many elementary school or even kindergarten students occupy a single room, of course, the real challenge for the teacher is trying to prevent the class from turning into utter chaos.

Working with children requires much greater energy and resourcefulness than would be necessary with older students but perhaps the rewards of having a child almost spontaneously grasp an English word or grammatical concept thanks to the teacher's repeated examples make the effort worthwhile.

A child's progress in a language is even harder to measure than an adult's. Children can almost never be taught specific linguistic items. The best the teacher can do is invent games and activities where the child is functioning in an English environment.

Pre-pubescent children are very playful and enjoy cooperative activities. They usually can't comprehend or aren't interested in abstractions (especially explanations of grammar or vocabulary) requiring the almost exclusive use of concrete objects and activities (e.g., use of the object or at least a picture of it for each vocabulary item). Most of all, they are very easily bored if they are not enjoying the activity and aren't challenged by it.

One sociologist believes that compared to their Western counterparts, Japanese kids under 8 years of age are considerably less disciplined. From 8 to 13 they seem more disciplined, although even at this age, discipline will be a problem, especially for a foreign instructor who can't express her demands to the students in Japanese. Unfortunately, schools have no concept of "combat pay" and salaries for teachers of children are comparable to those of teachers of adults.

What are realistic expectations about how much English a child can learn? Given an atmosphere of trust where the child feels safe to err, it shouldn't be too difficult to allow the young student to:

* Overcome nervousness with foreigners
* Acquire the sounds of English
* Recognize common English loan words
* Learn letters, numbers and vocabulary
* Acquire basic patterns of English grammar

To achieve these goals alone should give any teacher a feeling of genuine accomplishment and pleasure at knowing that such a competent child, in sharp contrast to his uninitiated schoolmates, will probably always have a special affinity, fondness and talent for English.

# Living and Teaching in Korea

At the risk of exposing my plebeian taste in the performing arts, I nevertheless have to say Korea reminds me of a *Star Trek* episode. Remember the one about the two aliens who duke it out on the *Enterprise*? Supposedly, their beef is based on some sort of prejudice (didn't you love how every show had a moral?) but no one could figure out why they hated each other when they both looked identical. Finally, the starship voyagers realized that while one guy was black on the right half of his body and white on the left, the other alien was white on the right and black on the left. Big deal.

So it is with Korea and Japan, I think. This chapter will certainly win me no friends in either country but the truth is, these two look and act like brothers (well, maybe cousins) who both insist the other was adopted. Each will tell you they have absolutely nothing in common but one week in both countries will show you that even the quintessentially "unique" aspects of the cultures are shared: *sushi* is *kimbap*, *sumo* is *ssirum* and *kibun* or the supposedly inscrutable "mood" that is the soul of either culture is even the same word in both languages.

What this means in practical terms is that if you like Japan, you'll feel pretty comfortable in this less frantic, perhaps somewhat more welcoming country whose people, renown for their love of drink and song, are sometimes called "The Irish of the Orient." While the Japanese are getting increasingly prickly about the number of *gaijin* trying to cash in on their country's material success, the Korean's are still quite respectful and friendly toward teachers from the Great Beyond.

The popular cliche that Korea is Japan 20 years ago may have been true until the 1988 Olympics. Then the economy got kicked into high gear and the gap seemed to close by about five years. Today, Seoul's 11 million people are hell-bent on getting the good life as quickly as possible, which, much to the consternation of their government economists, has meant they're starting to act like those irresponsible Westerners spending money they don't have.

Since 1990, the Korean economy has run a trade deficit just like America. Officially, this has been attributed to increased competition for cheap Asian labor, greater imports at Western insistence and a shortage of skilled labor. But unofficially, everyone knows that the Koreans went on a major spending spree in the last few years after winning big wage increases. Those higher wages meant higher prices for exports and less savings for investment so the economy tanked. Still, with growth at over 8% (compared with America's 3%), it's not a very deep tank.

Jobs are plentiful in the country whose workaholics put the Japanese to shame. Like the Japanese, Korean companies focus on exports and the people seem enamored of all things foreign. Studying English is considered a very practical, yet fashionable, activity--especially if your teacher is a white Westerner.

The Koreans have had plenty of practice meeting foreigners--usually on the battlefield. Throughout their 5,000-year history, there has almost always been some foreigner trying to dominate them. The bad blood between the Japanese and Koreans, for example, dates back to at least 1592 when the world's first ironclad warship was used to help send the Nipponese packing. Apparently the ship's dragon head complete with fire-breathing special effects was just too much for the ostensible "trade negotiators" from Rising Sun Inc.

Finally, in the early 17th Century, Korea declared itself a "closed country" (just like Japan, again) earning it the sobriquet "The Hermit Kingdom." Its Black Ships having successfully gotten the Japanese to start trading, the US failed to open Korea. Finally the Japanese got through in 1876, however, with the Americans following in 1882 and the Brits in 1883. The Japanese army invited itself in in 1894 to help the Korean government deal with a suspiciously convenient peasant uprising. That "help" made Korea a protectorate of Japan in 1905 and by 1910, Korea was a colony.

A lot of older Koreans speak excellent Japanese because, for all intents and purposes, Korea was a part of Japan until 1945. Atrocities during the war were plentiful, of course, and included such incidents as slave labor being exported to help keep war-ravaged Japanese factories running and the drafting of Korean "comfort girls" to keep Japanese soldiers company on the front lines. (Both these issues have been the subject of vast discussion, apologies and compensation but discrimination against third and fourth-generation Korean-Japanese living in Japan still as foreigners remains a source of tension.)

The country's split along the 38th Parallel came about when Papa Joe Stalin made the same cheap grab for Korea that he pulled in Japan when he declared war on atom-bombed Tokyo, snatching the country's northern islands. But in the case of Korea, his Russian troops beat the Americans in by about a month at the end of World War II in August 1945 and promptly set about absorbing the country into the USSR.

Finally, three years later, the two superpowers agreed to disagree by splitting the ancient country across the middle, making the Democratic People's Republic of Korea north of the 38th Parallel and the Republic of Korea south of it.

The divorce didn't help much. On June 25, 1950, the North Korean army came charging over the border, prompting a massive, coordinated response by 16 countries in the form of the UN Command (translation: the USA). By the end of the bitter fighting in 1953, much of the South lay in ruins; Seoul was little more than rubble.

Today, in contrast to the doors swinging wide in the rest of the formerly Communist world, the North remains the last remnant of the "Hermit Kingdom." Visitors are most definitely unwelcome and such impolite behavior as blowing up four South Korean cabinet officials in Rangoon and boring three tunnels big enough for tanks under the DMZ have kept relations with the South a wee bit cool.

So cool, in fact that South Korea is kept at a fairly high state of military preparedness, dishing out 35% of its national budget on defense and putting all young men in uniform for three years while over 50,000 US GIs help keep the fragile peace. As tensions in other parts of the world have eased, relations between the communist North and rich South remain frigid, especially in light of the North's ambitious nuclear bomb program. Maybe it's the threat of nuclear obliteration and tank-filled tunnels that keeps the people of the South working hard...and wages high!

In fact, in terms of actually putting money in the bank, teaching pay today in Korea rivals Japan. Check your newspaper for current exchange rates, but you'll probably be getting about 750 won for your US dollar. This means that at an hourly pay of between 10 and 15,000 won, your annual gross pay for a 30-hour week will be about $20,000, or approximately 3 times the average Korean salary. But what makes this otherwise uninspiring sum a lot more attractive is that although it changes annually depending on the current appetite of the government, income tax is astoundingly low in Korea--less than 5%. Thus almost everything you make goes straight to the bank (or bar, boutique, bistro or whatever).

In talking to teachers, I discovered several recent college grads who were putting away $1500 a month--without, I was assured, living in a rat hole or working themselves into a coronary. One 24 year-old from Wisconsin admitted that, after one year, "Korea is getting on my nerves. I find homogeneous cultures to be too sheltered; these Koreans certainly are." But, he reflected, "I must say that I'm making good money for easy work and good hours. I'm also loving the *taekwando!*"

Many young teachers say about $500 a month is enough for a comfy life even in Seoul. Well, maybe. But I suspect if you like a few creature comforts, you should plan on 50% more, still leaving enough for good savings and plenty of good times. After all, if the Koreans can regularly put away 1/3 of their meager earnings (which they indeed do to provide for their old age or to buy a house), you can certainly save a good chunk of your princely wages.

Now for the catch. Readers familiar with the housing situation in Japan probably think there could be no more tenant-unfriendly system than "key money." There is and it's called *wolsei*, your new colorful cultural quirk from hell.

Being perhaps the greatest savers on earth, the Koreans almost all have fairly hefty bundles of cash at their disposal. Those wishing to rent apartments are required to put a good bit of that cash in the hands of the landlord. The good news is that every won you hand over comes back when you leave (sans any repair costs for damage, of course). The bad news is that *wolsei* typically allows the landlord to ask for 10 to 15% of the property's *total* value. In real money, to get into a decent 300 to 350,000 won/month apartment, that's often about five million won in up-front cash. Ouch.

The owner, of course, makes off with the 15% interest he'll probably earn on the money while, at the end of your stay, you get back money devalued by Korea's roughly 8% inflation. Not a terrible deal compared to Japan's three or four month's lost "key money" but, of course, most of us heading off to a teaching stint abroad don't have quite that much spare change to toss into the pot.

Fortunately, most English schools in Korea understand the problems transient teachers face and are often willing to put up the *wolsei*. In the unlikely event your sponsoring school won't do that for you, shared apartments are quite common with two or three teachers living together, one of whom has an employer generous enough to let the others off the hook. (Note: Millionaire teachers may wish to consider the "wolsei" alternative: *jonsei*--paying a year's rent in advance. Doing so might get you free parking for your limo, who knows?)

English schools sometimes try to get teachers to stay in one of their "officetels" (hotel, motel, officetel--cute, huh?) These are generally featureless flats perched atop shops or offices. Although the areas are usually convenient and the rent may be less than similar standard apartments, be sure you find out how the utilities are paid. Too many officetels evenly split the month's lump-sum electric bill for the whole building. This is great if you're "Mr. Kim's TV Superstore" but a bit of a rip-off if you're a solitary English teacher--especially when you consider that Korean electricity rates are two to four times America's.

Another long-term living possibility is the same as the short-term solution: *yogwans*. These Korean-style hotels are relatively cheap (6-10,000 won/night) and owners are always eager to please long-stay guests with hefty discounts by the month. (For new-arrivals, however, I recommend the hostels noted in the Appendix as the best way to get plugged into the information grapevine and make friends fast.)

Foreign "ghettos" all tend to cluster around the huge Yongsam US Army base in Seoul. Itaewon is a popular spot due to its easy access to downtown schools and nearby burger joints. The overwhelming Americana displayed at every turn, however, (not to mention the presence of hundreds of "shop-til-you-drop" tourists all feverishly ferreting out discount Nikes) can be a bit offputting to those not into cultural chauvinism. The UN Village, Hannam-dong, and Namsan are also convenient but pricey. Far better for value and sanity is Dongbinggo-dong and nearby Riverside and Shindong Ah apartments which are not only reasonably priced but can be rented by the month--no *wolsei.*

Wherever you settle, however, make sure you're near one of the city's four excellent subway lines or at least served by busses. Unlike the approximately 5,000 US military guys and gals in Seoul, you won't have access to taxpayer-subsidized cheap gasoline so it's unlikely you'll get a car. Taxis (which always want to know how far you're going before they'll let you in and often stop to pick up extra passengers) are not always there when you need them.

Life is fairly comfortable in Korea, especially for Americans in Seoul where all the goodies from home are available. Stateside news fills the *Korea Times, Korea Herald, Korea Daily, USA Today* and the US military mouthpiece, the *Stars and Stripes.* The first three newspapers often have ads for teachers and sometimes ads for apartments which, if you can afford $7,500 to $10,000 *a month,* you might want to know about. (Such expatriate palaces are usually 90% subsidized by the expat tenant's deep-pockets company.)

Medical care is affordable and English-speaking hospitals are abundant in major cities, especially Seoul. Most employers do not provide health insurance so getting traveler's insurance before you leave home would be advisable. The International Clinic in Hannam-dong (tel.

796-1871) near UN Village is open 24 hours a day and everyone speaks English. Other hospitals catering to foreign residents include the Cheil, Severance, Kang Dong, Song Shim and the Seoul Choongang hospital.

If you're thinking of bringing your kids to Korea, be prepared to pay plenty to keep them in a Western-style school system--just think of it as their starting college a few years early. Liberty Christian School in Ui Jongbu 40 minutes from Seoul (PO Box 23, Ui Jongbu, Kyunggi-do, Korea 480-600; tel. 0351-872-3267) caters to military families. Korea Christian Academy in Taejon (210-1 O-Jung Dong, Taejon 300-210; tel. 042-622-3663) is fully accredited and charges accordingly. Seoul Academy (Young Dong PO Box 85; tel. 555-2475) emphasizes bilingual education and the three Rs. Seoul American School (APO San Francisco CA 96301; tel. 7918-5994) is operated by the US government and so gives priority to military kids. Seoul Foreign School (55 Yonhi-dong, Seodaemoon-ku; tel. 335-5101) is top-notch as is Seoul International School (Kangdong PO Box 61; tel. 233-4551) which sits on a gorgeous 7.5-acre campus. At any of these schools your wee one will get a great international education but all bets are off as to how big a nest egg you'll go home with. Then again, who ever said raising kids was supposed to be cheap?

Right after you pick all the necessary maps and guides from the Korea National Tourist Center (tel. 757-0086) near the Lotte Hotel in downtown Seoul, you should probably head over to one of the bigger bookshops in town to pick up more detailed information. They're located quite near the larger English schools in Chong-ro and so would make a convenient stop prior to interviewing. The Kyobo Bookstore near the Sejong Cultural Center, and the Chongro Bookstore opposite the YMCA are the most popular but the Royal Asiatic Society in the Christian Broadcasting Building seems to offer the best cultural works. Drop by the USO near Sookmyung University too for paperback book exchanges, US airline reservations and great greaseburgers just like back home. You needn't be one of America's finest to enjoy the facilities.

Laugh if you will at the thinly-disguised propaganda, but don't be too quick to knock the US military in Korea. Their presence will provide you with AM and FM stereo radio as well as the Armed Forces Korea Network TV station. Yes, friends, you can teach English in Korea *and* come home to David Letterman each and every weeknight (if you live in Seoul, that is). You can even enjoy him on your TV from home—the broadcasting systems and the electricity are US-compatible.

As is usually the case when working abroad, visas are a dicey business. As in Japan, employers like to personally inspect the merchandise before they make a commitment. The director of one of Seoul's top language schools, however, told me he might hire based on a video-taped sample lesson so as to check the candidate's appearance, accent and manner. In exchange for promising anonymity, he confided that in teaching, "education is *not* the key. Presentation is everything...Half the time the teacher will be 'babysitting' so, as long as you have a nice personality, you can make things work for you."

It is possible to teach in Korea even without a university degree. Certainly, the old sheepskin helps land the plum jobs and will certainly make the government look more favorably on your work visa application, but there are hundreds of people working legally (often on a student visa while studying some aspect of the culture) and not-so-legally. Even with more foreigners going over to teach these days, I would still recommend even non-grads give it a try. Even if nothing pans out with any of Seoul's 300-plus schools (hard to imagine), there's always Pusan, Taegu, Inchon, Kwangju, Taejon, Kyonggi, Chollanam, Kyongsangbuk and Kyongsangnam--all cities of over one million with dozens of English schools each.

Nine times out of ten, teachers will have to go to Korea on a tourist visa. Then, like the Japan of yore, teachers are obliged to leave the country to change to a working visa which will take about one month. Although a combination of lazing on the beach and trekking in the Golden Triangle draws many to Thailand, most teachers on a visa run just hop an express bus to Pusan (faster, cheaper and more frequent than trains) then a ferry to Osaka, which has a Korean consulate. Total round trip costs under US$200 and there's always the chance of doing some substitute teaching in Osaka while you wait. (See my book, JOBS IN JAPAN for a complete list of Japanese hostels and more English schools.)

Although not required, it pays to get your tourist visa before you leave home. If you just show up in Korea, you'll be given 15 days as a tourist. If you get a tourist visa at home, you'll be given a 60-day visa, good for multiple-entries for four or five years. Brits are good for 90-day stays.

Also like rich or nearly-rich countries everywhere, Immigration authorities are making things difficult for those trying to earn an honest buck in a slightly less-than-honest way. Working while on a tourist visa has always been illegal obviously, but for years Immigration turned a blind eye toward the doings of foreigners since they were not thought of as taking work from the natives. But with large numbers of poor Asians from such countries as the Philippines, Indonesia and China pouring in, authorities in the area's industrialized countries have started making things difficult for all foreigners.

If Immigration finds you working on a tourist visa, you can expect to pay a fine in the neighborhood of 100,000 won while your employer will pay many times more. Obviously, this is little more than a slap on the wrist monetarily but it does put you on the authorities' "naughty foreigner" list which could earn you deportation after too many such transgressions. It doesn't happen often--just enough to keep most tourists honest.

Not the least bit surprisingly, Korean students are very similar to the Japanese so Korean employers are looking for the same qualities as their Japanese counterparts. This means someone who is lively, personable, more-or-less attractive and maybe, just maybe, knows something about teaching English. The ideal age seems to be 25 to 34 although younger and older types will certainly find work if they can assure the director they are responsible and adaptable, respectively.

The Koreans seem to be not quite as far along in their understanding of the West's multi-ethnicity as Japan. Koreans often expect their English teachers to be white, suspecting minority teachers (especially Asian, even Korean) of speaking inferior English. Some schools are attempting to change this by consciously hiring minorities but there still seems to be resistance from students. In honesty, all non-white teachers should expect some discrimination while African Americans, because of the anti-Korean aspects of the Los Angeles riots of Spring '92, should be prepared for major problems.

One man trying to raise the Korean consciousness a bit is John Valentine, Program Director for Jong-Ro Foreign Language Institute in Seoul. Married to a Korean and fluent in the language, John goes out of his way to bring as much diversity to his teaching staff as possible. "It's been a struggle," he admits, "but my boss has allowed me to hire minority English teachers and not just lily-white ones. I just tell him to explain to the students that American society today is a rainbow." A good man to know in Seoul English circles, John has generously offered to do what he can to help newcomers of any color get plugged into the Korean system. Write or call him at the Jong-Ro school whose address is in the Appendix.

Compared to the Japanese, Korean students are livelier in class. Explained one delighted teacher while comparing the two groups, "The Korean kids *talk* to me!" Those visitors who know both cultures often say the Koreans are more emotional and perhaps aggressive. Certainly, Korea is a far more conservative society than today's Japan.

Fortunately so for teachers. The Koreans still adhere to the five traditional hierarchical relationships found throughout Asia: ruler/subject, parent/child, husband/wife, teacher/student and elder/younger. Of course, most students realize that the average foreign teacher has little if any real training for the work but still, they respect the teacher's position and the concept of study. Older teachers especially are revered (which is not to say preferred) and the frequently heard question "How old are you" has been known to irritate many an aging free-spirit. In fact, the inquirer is just trying to see how respectful he needs to be with you. (I usually just tell them I'm really 22 but afflicted with a horrible premature aging disease which I hope can be successfully treated with the Kimchi Wonder Diet...)

Incredible though it sounds, the Koreans are even more fanatical about learning than the Japanese. Like their Eastern nemesis, the Koreans say if a high school student sleeps more than four hours a night, he's not studying hard enough to pass the entrance exam. In the Korean's case at least, it's probably true. There are approximately three times the number of applicants for available university spots.

The society is brutally competitive and only the strong survive. Just ask a Vietnam veteran about the legendary discipline of the Korean troops who fought alongside the Americans and you'll get some sense of how tough the people's spirit is. Children rarely know their parents' names--it's always just "Mother" and "Father." People often feel uncomfortable about using first names which are generally reserved for intimate relationships with friends, family or lovers. But most importantly, a sense of decorum and dignity is necessary to maintain the key element of Korean culture: _kibun_ or a feeling of spiritual harmony. It's all fine in theory, of course, but the number of hot-heads you meet in Korea will make you wonder if anyone else has ever even heard of the concept.

Although the society is not blighted by bad English to the same degree as Japan, "Konglish" can sometimes perplex teachers and frustrate students. Like most English-speaking Asians, Korean students usually know English grammar very well and often have astoundingly good vocabularies, thanks to having studied the language since their early teens. The odds are good, however, that your English class will be the first time they have ever been expected to actually use the language for communication. Consequently, the biggest problem for them is a lack of confidence due to a lack of prior meaningful conversation.

Other English problems they have include pronunciation because of the Korean language's limited sound repertoire. The _"p/f"_ and _"l/r"_ sound pairs are especially tricky for them while articles, prepositions, the present perfect and the present continuous cause conniptions in the classroom. It's not that the tenses don't exist in Korean but that their language permits more "mistakes"--unlike the very strict rules of English grammar.

Class size is typically 12 students in a conversation class (the type you're most likely to teach) but 50 or even 60 in a grammar class which is usually handled by a Korean teacher. $> ^{\$}1,065.^{00}$ con

Many schools will pay sponsored teachers about a million won a month for a 30-hour work week and throw in a free minuscule apartment. One top-notch school, "Pagoda" in Seoul, however, pays its 18 foreign teachers about 11,000 per 50 minute session with raises every six months. The minimum work load is four classes per day rising to a maximum of eight. Monthly incomes of 1.5 million won are typical.

Although accommodations are not given to the teacher, the office staff helps find something reasonable, puts up the *wolsei* when necessary and provides basic furniture. In exchange for a one-year contract, round-trip airfare is provided. Pagoda management emphasizes, however, that they like to hire locally and usually only experienced teachers.

While teaching in Korea, it would certainly be worthwhile to learn a bit of the language which is becoming more and more common throughout Asia. One great plus the language has over Japanese and Chinese is the extensive use of *hangul*, a synthetic writing system invented and implemented by King Sejong in 1445. The 24-letter alphabet is said to be the most scientific and logical writing system in practical use today so learning it even before you go shouldn't be too tough. What tends to complicate one's reading prowess, however, is that the people also sprinkle liberal bits of their 1,800 character *Hanja* alphabet which is used to spell Chinese words in everyday usage.

Luckily, learning the spoken language is not just for rocket scientists. Korean belongs to the Ural-Altaic family of languages along with Finnish and Turkish. There are no articles and no real verb-subject agreement. Like Japanese (but unlike standard English), Korean conversation tends to be very forgiving with grammatical mistakes.

Still, if your Korean doesn't bridge the linguistic gap and you're feeling panicky, you can always fall back on English to resolve the crisis by calling a helpline: in Seoul, 735-0101; in Pusan: 051-44-0101; in Kyongju: 056-13-0101; and in Cheju: 064-46-0101. In general, however, I've learned that you can always find some kind soul nearby who speaks English well enough to help smooth your way--and who just might turn into a new friend!

# Living and Teaching
# in Taiwan

Few people going to Taiwan for the first time understand the unique politics of the country and the resulting mentality of the people. Most of us Asia-wanderers assume the Holland-sized island at a Mexican latitude is just another mini-dynamo of the Pacific Rim whose customs and language happen to be Chinese. Take a closer look though, and you realize the country's identity isn't merely a Chinese gloss. Taiwan *is* China--one side of a China suffering from severe schizophrenia.

Most foreigners have stopped calling the place "Formosa" (from the opinion of 16th Century Portugese explorers that the island was "the best") but there is, in fact, no country called "Taiwan" either. Both governments which claim the island agree that it is only a province. Where the Communists in Beijing and the Nationalists in Taipei disagree mightily is who should be controlling that big piece of real estate to the west.

Chinese history up to 1949 is essentially the same according to both the Communist People's Republic of China (PRC) and Taiwan's Republic of China (ROC). Neither was sad to see the Japanese booted out of Taiwan in 1945 after 50 years of colonization of the place. Then, after four years of fighting Mao's band in the power vacuum that followed Japan's defeat, the Nationalists, led by Chiang Kai-shek, decided that retreat from Chairman Mao's advancing army would be the better part of Chinese valor. Taking a lesson from the Brits at Dunkirk during World War II, the "Generalisimo" fled with about 2 million members of his still-formidable army and their families 100 miles across the Taiwan

Straits (barging in on a somewhat startled 8 million native Taiwanese) to await the Final Battle.

The Communists probably wouldn't have had much trouble taking Taiwan as well and finally smashing Chiang's Kuomintang (KMT) party. What Mao realized he *would* have had trouble with was America's Seventh Fleet which, in 1950, President Truman parked in the middle of the Straits. Although the rescue came a bit late in the game, the assistance has made Americans even today very popular with a grateful Taiwan public.

What followed was 25 years of military bristling and what *The Economist* magazine has called a "political fantasy" with tiny Taiwan claiming to be the one true government of mainland China. Finally, of course, it became obvious that the Communists were there to stay and that the KMT's claim to Beijing was a little farfetched. In 1971, the UN made the ROC hand over its membership to the Communists and Taiwan found itself alone in a hostile world.

Say what you will about Tricky Dicky but President Nixon was the first to move the world into reality vis-a-vis the Chinese. By going to Beijing in 1972, he opened the door between China and the West. But his recognition of the Communists as the one true Chinese government, consequent closing of Taipei's US Embassy and abrogation of the US-ROC security treaty in 1979 left Chiang and company once again waiting for the Red Fleet to come steaming over the horizon.

It might well have done so if Taiwan hadn't been so rich and China so poor. No one knows for sure, of course, but the popular reason for the Communists not gobbling up little Taiwan when not much stood in the way is that China needed a doorway to the West (and the friendship of the West) more than it needed to pillage Taiwan's wealth. Then, too, the West's abandonment of the KMT was a bit of a sham. Despite the fact that 31 major countries closed their embassies in Taiwan when they opened them in Beijing, they all turned right around and simultaneously set up special "representative offices" which, of course, are embassies in all but name.

Today, despite no formal change in their identical position (termed officially, "one China, two areas), the two governments are getting along swimmingly, proving conclusively that people busy getting rich don't have time to make war. Big Taiwan companies have already sunk US$2 billion into setting up low-wage plants in China, since 1988, family relatives have been flowing back and forth across the Straits and the streets of both capitals are filled with Big Mac-munching yuppies.

There's really no clearer proof of the failure of Communism than to look at the difference between the PRC and the ROC. Until the split, the average income was about US$100 a year. In the PRC, it still is; in Taiwan, it's up to about US$8,000. With mounds of exports and only a few imports, the country is sitting on the largest pile of foreign reserves in the world: US$76 billion. What makes this feat of frugality especially amazing is that the government has had to pay about 11% of everything the country makes for defense—twice America's ratio and over 10 times Japan's ratio. Clearly, Taiwan-style capitalism works and, just as with Hong Kong, the Communist Chinese have obviously decided to leave well enough alone and get on with the business of business.

It's no mystery, of course, why the world's biggest success stories have been the countries of East Asia where education is seen by even ordinary citizens as critically important. Anthropologist Robert Redfield thinks this love of education is only one of the traditional habits of the "Little Tradition" which is largely based on Confucian thought. Along with education, he says, Orientals generally support family cohesion, hard work, frugality and saving, respect for authority, competition for wealth and position, a mercantile view of the world and using the society's educated elite as arbiters of taste. Certainly not all values we in the West would support but the great wealth of the area does give one ideas as to how we could get ourselves back on track, eh?

As a quick inspection of the underside of almost any medium-tech bit of plastic wizardry will attest, Taiwan's business is light manufacturing. Unlike the Japanese and Koreans, the Chinese don't seem able or interested in building massive corporations like the *zaibatsu* or *chaebol*. Instead, they tend to recruit brothers, aunts, second cousins and in-laws to make family-based companies which can only grow as big as their "relative" size. Some international economists think this unwillingness to think big will someday be Taiwan's undoing but, for now, the good times are rolling.

So good are the times right now that a large labor shortage has developed. In 1990, there were about four times as many jobs offered as there were applicants at state-run employment agencies. Of course, not all such jobs are plums. As in all rich countries (but perhaps most especially in the *nouveau riche* "Little Dragons" of Asia), there is a general disdain these days for any sort of work involving, well, *work*. With average wages growing by more than 10% each year in the early '90s and unemployment under 2%, people can afford to be quite picky about their employment. The grubbiest jobs nowadays are often left to the estimated 60,000 foreign "guest workers" eager to escape their less-enlightened governments. The best jobs today require facility with the World Language, English--which is where you come in.

As Taiwan's role in the international community has increased, the need for English has kept pace. Today's Taiwanese businessmen (and increasingly, women) travel and correspond throughout the world to spread their wares and in every dealing with a *lau wai* (foreigner), English is the language used, even with other Asians. As elsewhere, studying English is seen as the best ticket to a better life and a very fashionable activity where, as the saying has it, "education is inferior to all else."

As elsewhere in Asia, students have a good fundamental grasp of English grammar and vocabulary, having studied English since they were at least 13. What they need as adults and can really only get from a native speaker is practice using English for communication. Teaching such "conversational English" usually consists of little more than the teacher asking the students to explain to her the little mysteries of the culture that have been puzzling her since her arrival. And they call this work?

In fact, the students' grasp of grammar is not quite as good as they would like to think. Once you enter the classroom, you'll find serious holes in their use of articles, plurals, subject-verb agreement, prepositions and verb tense. On the other hand, having learned the 7000 characters necessary to read the average Taiwan newspaper, who can blame them for having slouched through an English class or two?

At least half of the students you'll teach will be in high school or college, preparing for their next round of "examination hell" which determines who gets to go to which prestigious school and who is left behind. Another 30% might be adults to include business types and housewives while the remaining 20% might be kids whose eager parents have put them in a conversational English class to give them a leg up on their scholastic competitors.

The choicest jobs are invariably at universities and because they are tops in terms of hours and pay, they generally go to those who've been around long enough to have the right connections. You'll probably start your teaching at a _bushiban_--private schools run very much for profit, generally not too particular about a teacher's background, especially if they're on a tourist visa, which is often the case.

Most schools will expect you to have a four-year university degree but, in fact, few ask about it and fewer still expect any documentation. Before hiring, some will ask you to perform a sample lesson but many will simply check to see if you're breathing. If so, you've got the job.

North Americans have the easiest time getting hired because it's the brand of English the students all clamor for in this Yankee-loving land. (Even President Lee chose to get his PhD at Cornell.) Brits, especially, might want to consider equally-wealthy Hong Kong or Singapore for their teaching as those countries often prefer the King's English. In Taiwan, on the other hand, it's said that some schools make their teachers tell the students they're American whether it's true or not.

Likewise, many Chinese will affect English first names to appear more "international." It's true this makes the person's name easier for a Westerner to pronounce and remember but it does make for some awkward moments when the young lady you've just been entranced by introduces herself with a straight face as "Kitty Chow."

Prime teaching time is weekday evenings, from 6 to 9 p.m. when students are able to come straight to class from their work. Wednesday and Saturday afternoons are reportedly good for children's classes where youngish female teachers are preferred. As in other Asian countries, weekday afternoons may be tough to fill with teaching work if you're free-lancing it, so it's good to have some part-time writing work lined up to keep you busy during your down time.

Much to the delight of most Westerners working in Taiwan, the New Taiwan Dollar (NT$) has appreciated about 60% against the US$ since 1984.

Today, you can expect to pay just 25 NT$ (locally called *kuai*) for each US$. At $250 to $1,000 ($500 is typical) per hour of teaching and low living costs, you can be sure that you'll have a very tidy pile of NT$ to deal with when it comes time to head home. In fact, most teachers are able to save from US$1,200-$1,500 a month.

Dress in the tropics is usually casual to keep people from keeling over when the temperature and humidity both head for triple-digits (worst from June to September). Lucky for you, teaching attire in Taiwan schools is much less formal than Japan or Korea. No suits here, just a nice pair of slacks and short-sleeved shirt. Keep things neat and clean, of course, and steer clear of blue jeans and scruffy tennis shoes (definitely no shorts, sandals or T-shirts).

The best time to get a good reception is just before each new semester's start (i.e., September and February). Early February is also favorable because of Chinese New Year when people implement their New Year's resolutions which, short-lived though they may be, often include, "this year really getting serious about learning English." July and August can also be a good time for job hunting as regular schools are out and students often head for the *bushiban* to bone up for next year. (*bushiban* is not the correct spelling according to the Wade-Giles romanization system Taiwan (but not the PRC) uses but it is at least pronounceable for non-Mandarin speakers).

Unfortunately, as is often the case in that part of the world, style wins out over substance and how a teacher looks and acts often count far more than how good a job he can do in the classroom. Minority Westerners may experience discrimination as will older people who may be seen as less able to relate to young students and get them talking freely. Still, there is a fair bit of student grumbling currently about apathetic and inexperienced teachers wasting class time so a person with a few years of experience (any experience) might be well-received. Teachers in their 30s and 40s seem to have no problem finding work.

Unlike many countries these days which allow tourists to just "drop in," all foreigners need to obtain visas before arriving in Taiwan. "Resident" (or working) visas are very difficult to obtain beforehand and most schools don't even offer them to their teachers. In general, you should request a renewable five-year "visitor's visa" good for two-months which, in theory, may be renewed twice in Taiwan for a total stay of six months. Staying more than six months requires leaving the country to reset the visa clock for another six-month span.

Renewals in country, however, are not automatic. You've got to provide Immigration with a plausible reason for wanting to stay longer. "Yes," they'll say, "we understand you love the natural beauty of Taiwan and want to learn more about our ancient and fascinating culture, but don't you think it's about time you went back to your Mom?"

Experience has shown that the best (if not only) reply to this gambit is to whip out your letter from the school where you're studying Chinese for a minimum of ten hours per week. Very few of the hundreds of foreigners studying Chinese get a proper student visa because they are generally granted only for degree programs. Consequently, no one really knows (or apparently cares) how many of the island's Chinese language students are really keen on learning the language and how many are using it as a ticket to teach. The point is, it makes your reason for renewing credible.

It is possible to do things legally, of course, and get a resident visa which can have real advantages over being a tourist. For one thing, as a resident, you're able to open a bank account and transfer money (other than traveller's checks) overseas. For another, as a resident, you're almost certain to stay more than six months, entitling you to the "resident tax rate" of around six percent of your income. Until you've been in Taiwan more than six months, you'll get socked with a 20% withholding tax on your pay, a good bit of which will be refunded if and when you stay longer.

Unfortunately, because of the large number of Asian "guest workers" overstaying their visas, Immigration is making things difficult for us all. Even if a school wants to sponsor you, the government, of course, reserves the right to decide who gets official permission to work (with a resident visa). In general, you'd probably need a four-year degree, some sort of TESL/TEFL training and at least two-year's teaching experience to qualify as a "foreign expert." Most teachers don't bother and most *bushiban* never sponsor. Still, you should do what you can to stay more than six months so you can get that tax refund of around 14% of your income.

Job listings sometimes appear in the *China Post* or the *China News* but most teaching gigs are found through word-of-mouth (hostels are hotbeds of info) or tacked to one of Taipei's English bulletin boards. Check out the Student Lounge at the Mandarin Training Center in Shi-ta (or National Taiwan Normal) University on Hoping East Road, the Stanford Center (a different "Mandarin Training Center") at the National Taiwan University on Shin-hai Road, or the TIYAC bulletin board at the Taipei International Youth Activities Center (which also features one of the city's best youth hostels) at 30 Hsin Hai Road, Section 3. You'll also find notices of all kinds posted at the *Mandarin Daily News* Office on Fu Chow Street. Lucky Bookstore (also at Shi-ta University) and Caves Bookstore are always a good place to meet teachers and reap the grapevine's latest fruit.

Life is no longer dirt cheap in most of Asia, certainly not in Taiwan. Still, if saving money is the name of your game, you can get by on about $15,000 a month. You should expect to pay about the same for rent as you would in an American city: between $5000 and $15,000 (bargaining is expected). Personally, I favor the strategy of finding a great place for cheap near a cemetery (the Chinese hate ghosts) but most teachers just opt for a furnished room in a shared apartment for about $5,000 or a room at their favorite hostel for about $4,000. Should you opt for an apartment, the good news is that Taiwan has no nightmarish "key money" system like Japan or Korea. Two month's refundable security deposit and your first month's rent and the place is yours.

Most foreigners wind up in one of the "ghettos" where shopkeepers know some English and locals don't stare at every white face they see. Shih Lin, for example, is across the river and is full of apartment buildings and shops catering to Westerners. It also has the biggest night market in Taipei making for fun shopping and street food. Wellington Heights in Peitou is perched on a hillside giving some nice views (for a price) but limited transportation makes commuting tough. The same problem applies to Yangminshan behind the Grand Hotel; it's popular with big-buck expatriate business-types but poor value for the budget teacher.

Some ambitious types head for Tienmu (a northern suburb) which, although pricey, features many Western amenities as well as prime hunting for well-heeled private English students willing to pay top *kuai* for their teacher's time. Check out the job and apartment listings in Tienmu at Jake's Country Kitchen, Taster's Restaurant, Gateway or the Community Services Center all on Chung Shan North Road.

Apartments are usually found by word-of-mouth but you'll see ads for them in shop windows, on telephone poles and, of course, at realtors, who will probably charge you 1/2 month's rent for the service. Be on the lookout for apparently abandoned houses still in good condition.

Asking around in the neighborhood could get you in at a very cheap (sometimes free) price.

Most apartments come with a stove and that's about all. Of course, some schools have basic furniture for new arrivals but you may have to scrounge for some yourself. One idea is to look for a place near a university. Students often come from out of town too so apartments which cater to them are often furnished with the essentials. Don't bother buying a shower curtain, though; the Taiwanese don't believe in them. As one student told me, "we think the bathroom _should_ get wet!"

Taipei has a subway planned for implementation around the turn of the century but long-time residents confess they're not sure _which_ century. Hopeless optimists note that Kaohsiung, Tainan and Taichung are also scheduled to have such systems but for these, no one even hazards a guess as to when _they'll_ be rolling. Until then, you'll probably be getting around town on the bus, which for a mere $10 will take you anywhere within the zone, after which you'll be asked to pay another fare. For $8000-$12,000, many teachers pick up a 125cc motorbike to help them zip around the ubiquitous traffic jams. (Bring a license from home and have it changed in Taiwan. Easy!)

Needless to say, whilst zipping through traffic, some zig when they should have zagged and so find themselves in need of medical attention. National Health Insurance covers only about half the population right now but the government is determined to make it universal in a few years. It's unclear as to whether or not foreigners will be eligible (they're not now) but, until it's decided, you'd do well to bring your own traveller's insurance from home. Medical fees are far less than in the West and you'll find plenty of excellent English-speaking hospitals. Some of the best known are: the Adventist Hospital on Pateh Rd. (tel. 771-8151), Mackay Memorial Hospital on Chungshan N.

Rd. (tel. 543-3535) and the National Taiwan University Hospital on Changten St. (tel. 312-3456).

Taipei will certainly win few awards for livability. It's three million people all seem to have motorbikes, none with mufflers. "Environmental awareness" is interpreted as knowing the best spot in the Tamsui River to pitch your rubbish where 30 years ago, you could actually drink the water. Still, as the country's economic and political center, Westerner work opportunities (teaching, writing, modeling, etc.) are unrivaled. It's also a cinch to get around the capital without speaking Chinese and women need have no worries about their safety, day or night.

The capital is also the country's fun center. The spectacular National Palace Museum has so many treasures from the mainland (over 600,000) that every visit is different. Good English collections at the American Club, the American Cultural Center, Gateway, the National Central Library and the Taipei Municipal Library will fill your reading needs easily. You'll find plenty of compatriots in Taipei as well at the American Club (tel. 594-8260), the Canadian Society (tel. 713-7268), the Australian/NZ Group (tel. 895-6460) and, for women, Our Place (tel. 871-2614). Check at Gateway or the Community Service Center for others.

Foreign films abound with English soundtracks intact and the Roxy Club near Shi-ta University offers up excellent home-grown rock-and-roll as does the city's all-English FM radio station, ICRT. You'll also probably spend a few evenings with MTV. No, not that one--*Movie* Television. You and your chums pile into a small room amply stocked with drinks and munchies and watch your favorite video (same system as America's). You'll also probably get dragged to a "KTV" joint one day. Give up? *Karaoke* Television, the reluctant crooner's nightmare come true.

For those not wishing to live in a Chinese version of "Blade Runner," however, the south might appear a bit more livable. Check around first to find out what industrial parks have been tossed up recently to relieve Taipei's congested manufacturing areas. Such places often need English speakers not only to teach staff but to help with foreign correspondence and product operating instructions. For starters, try the Shinchu Industrial Park which is said to pay better than Taipei schools and is a far more pleasant place to live.

Keelung, once a base for 16th Century Japanese pirates, is the only city north of Taipei, just 30 km by expressway. Because the city was occupied by the Spanish, Dutch and French also and still serves as a major harbor, Keelung retains an international feeling. Nice beaches, good camping, plentiful hot springs (all too often crammed on weekends with escaping Taipei-dwellers) and a sub-tropical climate averaging 72 degrees (22 Celsius) make for pleasant living conditions in this city of 350,000. If, that is, you don't mind a little moisture. It's said to be one of the rainiest cities in the world with buckets falling daily between October and March..

About 170 km south of Taipei on the West coast is Taichung, population 760,000. Also the site of a major harbor, it's home to about 20,000 manufacturers so you can assume business is foremost on the minds of these Formosans. On the one hand, this means English work is plentiful but, on the other, traditional Chinese culture is vanishing fast as "progress" attempts to bulldoze the city's many Chinese-style parks and pavilions. Aside from the Confucian Temple, there's not much good to be said about the city aside from its location in the middle of things. The spectacular mountains of Central Taiwan and the Lukang Historical Site's dozens of gorgeous old temples are easily reached from Taichung.

Further down the West Coast you'll find the 680,000 people of Tainan, 330 km from Taipei. The oldest city on the island, the 300-year-old buildings, some 300-odd temples and the occasional ox cart all give the place a great laid-back tropical feel and have earned it the moniker of "the Kyoto of Taiwan." Foreigners are few and housing deals abound. (One teacher got an entire old wooden Japanese-style house with garden for $3000 a month.) If you're into the beach-bum / culture-vulture scene, this may be the one for you.

Finally, continuing down to the end of the Sun Yat-Sen Memorial Freeway 348 km from Taipei, you'll find Kaohsiung which, with 1.4 million people, is Taiwan's biggest port and largest industrial center. Of course, this means that English work abounds but the quality-of-life could be better.

Summers are soggy in the south with monsoons blowing in steadily from July to September (when the north is nicest). Still, if you can handle living in distinctly tropical heat, the nearly deserted East coast of the island is easily accessible and the Central Mountain Range is less than an hour away. Here you'll find the fascinating Aboriginal Culture Park where, the government promises you can "conveniently observe aborigine culture." Think they have plans to build any "Foreigner Culture Parks"? If you do sign up as an exhibit, just make sure they pay you like a teacher!

# Common Student Errors

As a rule, Asian students have many of the same problems, a fact which makes teaching considerably easier than having to conduct an "error analysis" of each and every student's mistakes. This is not to say that each student doesn't have his own unique difficulties but the problem areas are, by and large, consistent across the board.

Robert Stockwell, a UCLA linguist has termed the categories of differences between languages as "split," "new," "absent," "coalesced," "reinterpreted," and "transferred." In the case of Japanese, Korean and Chinese student, these differences pose varying degrees of difficulty.

One of the biggest difficulties Japanese and most other Asian students have in pronunciation, for example, is distinguishing between two sounds where, in their own language, there may be only one. Most Japanese couldn't hear, let alone say, the difference between *coast* and *cost.* In Japanese, there's just one "*o*" sound. The student must learn to "split" the sounds in his mind.

Other sounds or grammatical structures (such as the articles *a, an,* and *the*) are completely absent in most Asian languages. These are "new." Particle markers which are common in Asia to indicate subject, object, possessives and others are simply "absent" from English.

On the other hand, there are some differences that the student can't merely ignore when he speaks English. Instead, the Japanese student must merge such things as the special counters for certain types of objects used in Japanese (e.g. *pon* for *bottles, satsu* for *books,* etc.) which are "coalesced" into the simple one, two, three of English.

Other times, the student may recognize the function of an English structure as being similar to a structure in his own language but it's still completely different and must be "reinterpreted." For example, the English auxiliary *do* serves the same function in questions as the Japanese and Korean *-ka* at the end of an interrogative sentence but it is different in form. Finally (and thankfully) there are some structures such as many of the consonant sounds which can be "transferred" from Oriental languages to English without change.

Mistakes in vowel sounds are very common among Asian students and may be a source of frustration for teacher and student alike. Major errors in this area are a result of either new sounds or "split" sounds. In order of difficulty, the new sounds which cause the most problems for Japanese and Koreans especially, are those such as *f, v, th* (as in *thick*), *th* (as in *then*), *l* and *r*.

Problems with split sounds include the contrast between the vowel sounds in, for instance, *hit/heat, hut/hat, cat/caught/coat, suit/soot.* Among consonants, you'll find your students saying *heat* for *feet, za* for *the* and *sank* for *thank,* probably because, as new sounds, they can't be heard without training.

Syntactically, students will make many mistakes as they try to transfer rules from their own language to English. The possessive *s* becomes an easy addition to any noun with which the Japanese would use their possessive particle *no.* "*Watakushi no hon*" becomes "*my's book.*"

Because there are no articles, no plural noun forms and no count or mass noun rules in Japanese, Korean or Chinese, the students will apply them in English frequently at random: *"those rices," "too many monies," "play much game."* The subjunctive is also new (in the Japanese subjunctive, there's no change in tense) so you'll hear lots of such things as, *"When I was boy, my father say if I don't graduate university, I can't take good job."*

Use of participles is in the split category as students need to differentiate between present and past participles: *"I was so exciting when the phone rang."* The passive always causes confusion too but mostly because it hasn't been drilled or explained adequately: *"I was enjoyed school and I was studied hard."*

For some reason, Oriental students love the infinitive, which is a new form for them: *"She enjoyed to study with him"* and *"We enjoyed to see it."* Paradoxically, when an infinitive would work perfectly well, many students will choose a gerund: *"I was asked for washing dishes"* and *"Then we went to spending allowance."*

Chinese, Japanese and Korean are fairly "lean" languages in that verbs frequently can be omitted when the context is clear. A famous Japanese *haiku* poem, for instance, illustrates a lack of grammar that would be inexcusable in English: "Mustard blossoms; moon in the east; sun in the west/Old pond; frog jumping; water's sound." Unfortunately, some students think their English should be so uncluttered by verbs, resulting in utterances like, *"He can English very well"* and *"He could everything at school."* We can understand him perfectly well, but alas, there are certain linguistic conventions that must be observed. English is much stricter about grammar than most of their spoken languages.

Mistaken use of prepositions include *at* for *in* or *on* for *to* (and vice versa), *in* for *on* or *to*, *of* for *in*, *on* for *in*, and liberal use of *from* for just about anything. The real problems with prepositions is that the Asian variety is usually considered part of the word it modifies. For this reason, many students don't even know what a preposition is and have a hard time learning to insert them where necessary.

Articles are altogether new for the Orientals who, quite logically, find them completely unnecessary and often can't believe we really use them even in casual speech. Amusingly enough, when the student finally realizes we're serious about putting these silly little "non-words" in front of nouns, he'll sprinkle them in his English with gusto. *"I like a fishing with the friends."* Anything to make the teacher happy!

English relies primarily on placement of words to keep meaning clear--the familiar "subject, verb, direct object" pattern. Word order is very flexible in Oriental languages such as Japanese and Korean, however, with word functions being defined by particles such as *wa, ga,* or *no* to let the listener know what's being said about whom.

So when your students try to speak English with the same loose rules about word placement that they're used to back home, you'll probably hear some real hodgepodge arrangements like; *"I must find where is my notebook," "On piano we can play," "They had white little dog,"* and *"I like very much them."* The only fixed position in Asian sentences is really just the final verb which always comes at the end of the sentence.

In Japanese, negation is always attached to the final verb at the end of the sentence. Consequently, negative pronouns like *no one, nobody* and *nothing* cause problems: *"Everybody don't come to party," "Anybody can't speak English."* And, just like most students of English all over the world, Asians have difficulty with subject-verb agreement: *"Some people spends too much time playing"* and *"Every man are hard worker."*

Vocabulary says a lot about any culture, especially what is important and what is alien. The Japanese, for example, have five different words for "rice:" *ine* for the rice plant, *momi* for rice grains, *kome* for cooking rice, *gohan* for cooked rice, and *mochi* for rice cake. I've always thought it interesting too that the words for clean and pretty are identical: *kirei.*

Aside from pure rote memorization of vocabulary, English vocabulary items that cause special grief for the average student include use of *house* or *home* instead of *family*, the distinction between *come* and *go* and *bring* and *take*, and several other minor translation errors.

To intensify, we use *more, most* or tack *-er* or *-est* to the end of the adjective being enhanced. The Oriental method is to repeat the adjective to add emphasis. Consequently, they will frequently say such things as, *"New Year's is the big, big holiday in my country"* or *"I live in a little, little house."*

Encourage (if not require) your students to purchase a good American or British-made English-only dictionary for use in class. Translation is rampant in most classes and is so deleterious to language learning that I forbid use of bilingual dictionaries in my classes. I think by using monolingual dictionaries, the students get the gist of the meaning just as effectively and are exposed to synonyms. They also avoid some of the outdated and just plain weird definitions that appear in bilingual English dictionaries.

Cultural differences regarding politeness can cause a fair bit of confusion. All Asian tongues pay much more attention to social position of the speaker vis-a-vis his listener. Japanese, for example, has three primary registers for talking to a superior, taking about oneself and talking to a young person or social inferior. Thanks to Western media, many students believe English has only one register: casual. This misconception needs to be corrected before the erring student starts asking his American boss, "what's happenin', dude?"

This concern for politeness also manifests itself in the way Asians respond to some yes-no questions. Whereas if a native speaker were asked *"You didn't go to school today, did you?"* he would probably reply (if he hadn't gone and wanted to be truthful), *"No,"* implying *"I didn't."* The Oriental, on the other hand, while trying to be truthful and focusing on the speaker not the question would probably reply, *"Yes,"* implying *"You are correct. I didn't go to school."*

This quirk of the cultures has been cause for numerous misunderstandings and even a few false accusations. Sure, you'll probably feel like you're in the middle of a "Who's On First" Abbott and Costello routine by the time you've gotten a straight answer but it's all part of the crazy fun that is TEFL. Patience, please!

# Tools of the
# Teaching Trade

English schools in Asia generally expect their teachers to have with them a collection of exercises, drills, activities and games to be used in conjunction with textbooks and general materials provided by the school. This "bag of tricks" often serves to liven up classes and allows the teacher to avoid overreliance on the texts. Although textbooks serve as useful "points of departure" for lessons, it is the teacher's own collection of meaningful articles, exercises and "realia" (everyday artifacts) that brings an English class to life.

Getting beyond dependence on the "basic five" classroom tools of teacher, students, blackboard, classroom and textbook can be difficult in a country where the teacher is unfamiliar with the language and the means to obtain audio-visual or other supporting materials. Explaining to your school what you need and how it will benefit students, however, should encourage your supervisor to assist you in your efforts to make classes more lively and valuable.

The following activities are a few suggested ways by which you can keep your students stimulated, entertained...and learning.

Games should be more than relief from the usual classroom routine. They can teach every bit as effectively as a drill and much more entertainingly. With games, English is used to accomplish a task and, as such, brings students closer to the real world where the language can be used for actual communication.

You can purchase quite a number of excellent games as well. You might want to obtain catalogs of classroom aids and games from such school suppliers as Remedial Education Press, 2138 Bancroft Place NW, Washington DC; Garrard Publishing, 1607 N. Market, Champaign, IL 61820; University of Michigan Press, Ann Arbor, Michigan; English Language Service, 5550 Wilkins Court, Rockville MD 20852 or Milton Bradley, Springfield, Mass. 01101.

The games presented here stress listening comprehension, vocabulary and communication skills (such as direction-giving). I have not included spelling games because too often these don't use the language in context. I really can't think of how a student's command of English is improved simply by coming up with as many words as possible that begin with the letter *b*.

Before the game begins, the class should practice sentence patterns and vocabulary likely to be encountered playing it. Explanation of the game should be thorough and a check should be made after explaining to ensure comprehension (e.g., "So, Ellen, what happens if somebody rolls a seven?"). Competition almost always heightens student interest when teams are created.

*Simon Says* (teaches imperatives)--students are instructed to perform an overt physical response (e.g., "Put your right hand on your head") or to draw something (e.g., "Draw a large circle with a small square inside"). To teach prepositions, the teacher may present increasingly complicated commands (e.g., "Put your pencil beside your notebook which you have put under Peter's coat." Of course, with true *Simon Says*, the student must remember to respond only when the teacher prefaces the command with "Simon says."

*Traveler Puzzle* (teaches note-taking, vocabulary, and listening comprehension)--Copies of a map showing towns, roads, railroads, a river, a lake and a mileage scale for a fictitious country are distributed to students. They are then told that a traveler must get from one point to another with only a certain amount of money or within a certain amount of time.

Students are then told about routes and transportation available and how much each costs (e.g., the train goes from Smallville to Pleasantburg at 50 mph and costs $20; a bicycle can be rented for travel between Pleasantburg and Mt. Hightop for $10 a day; etc.) Students then break into small groups to figure out what combination of transportation and what route would get the traveler to his destination on time and within his budget. As each group tries to be the first with the answer, the competitive spirit grows and careful monitoring becomes necessary to discourage use of the students' own language.

_Crossword Puzzles_ (vocabulary, relative clauses)--After the concept of crosswords is explained, blank copies of the crossword are given to students and clues are given orally to overly difficult words. It's best if student's names or personal activities can be worked into the activity; e.g., "Number 7 across: What Alex eats for breakfast every morning." A good exercise for advanced students is to create their own--in English only, of course!

_20 Questions_ (yes-no questions)--"It" is given a word or makes up one himself from a restricted category such as: objects in the room, any object, places, occupations, or people (living and dead). Other students then take turns asking up to 20 questions (in turn or as a group) that can only be answered _yes_ or _no_, and try to guess the word. Each student may either ask a question or make a guess. Scoring is possible by giving as many points to "it" as it took questions to guess his word.

_Charades_ (present continuous and simple past; vocabulary)--"It" is told or chooses his own activity and acts it out silently while the other students take turns trying to guess it using the structure being taught; e.g. "Are you _(verb) + ing?_" or "Did you *(verb)?*" You might want to form teams and time each side's efforts to add competition.

*Alibi* (past tense; reported speech)---The class is told that yesterday a bank was robbed and two suspects have been apprehended. They deny their involvement and claim to have been together at the time the crime was committed. Two volunteers from the class are then selected and told to leave the class to decide what their alibi will be.

After the remaining students have decided what questions to use in the interrogation, one "suspect" is brought back in and each student in the class asks one *wh-* question. The other student is then brought in and the same questions (perhaps asked by different students) are then posed. Responses are noted and all students compare them, pointing out discrepancies using reported speech; e.g., "Angela said they had eaten steak but Ellen said it was chicken."

*Definition* (relative and noun clauses; listening)--After the class has been divided into teams, representatives from each are given words written on pieces of paper. (Words should be of a category recently dealt with in a lesson, such as action verbs, adjectives, etc.) The team member then tries to define the word for her teammates without using the word or any of its derivatives. Time taken for the team to guess the word is recorded and the team with the least total time wins. A variation for advanced students has teams given lists of related words. Teams then try to guess as many of the words as possible within the allotted time.

*Password* (pronunciation)--The class is divided into teams and one student from each is sent out of the room where the teacher tells them a word. Back in class, the selected student gives one-word clues one at a time to each teammate in turn. Clues can be given only once to ensure the best possible pronunciation and can't be derivatives of the word to be guessed. As a group or individually, the team guesses the word after each clue. Score is kept by recording the number of clues necessary to guess each word with the lowest number winning.

*Concentration*--This game seeks to match words, either possessives with their pronouns, artifacts with occupations (*hammer* and *carpenter*), cardinal numbers with numerals, or any other relationship you can think of. On large pieces of paper, write your selection of any easily divisible number of, for example, occupational tools. Then, on index cards, write their respective occupations. Staple blank sheets over the sheets with names of tools and tape these on the board in rows and columns. Label the rows with numbers and the columns with good minimal pair letters such as *b, v, f, s, m, n,* etc.

Divide the class into teams. The teacher reads the word on the index card (e.g., "carpenter") and the team member must guess by calling out row and column where the corresponding tool is (e.g., a hammer). A correct guess wins another turn and that sheet from the board. Score is kept according to how many sheets each team has when the board is cleared.

*Picture Matching* (present continuous; articles)--The teacher assembles a collection of 5 to 10 similar photos or illustrations; e.g., people walking. Each student is given one without other students' seeing it and told to prepare a verbal description of it with the teacher's assistance. When all students have prepared their descriptions, each student tells his to the class. The other students take notes and remember which student said what. The photos are then mixed together and the teacher shows them one at a time to the group which then must try to match student with photo. Points may be awarded for correct guesses.

*Recipes* (articles, directions, vocabulary)--This is an especially fun game with female students but men can come up with some bizarre taste-treats too! The vocabulary of cooking is discussed with names of foods, spices and cooking techniques (such as baking, broiling, frying, etc.) presented. (Be sure the tough pronunciation items like *milk, lard* and *flour* get included too.) The teacher puts these on the board in categories then instructs teams to choose a sufficient number from each category to make the best dishes they can (usually with a total of ten ingredients). There may be several courses. Teams then tell the class how to prepare their creation and the class votes on the tastiest or most nauseating concoction. (Be prepared for the weird!)

*Neighbors* (prepositions, vocabulary)--A rather complex game, probably best-suited for advanced students, this can be very intellectually challenging and, if you're not careful, confusing for the teacher. First, on a grid, map out the names, ages, occupations, nationalities, type of house, type of car, family size and whatever other pertinent information you can think of for about six people living in the same neighborhood. Names should be listed vertically, the other qualifiers horizontally. Fill in each box; e.g., under Jack's family, write, "two daughters," under Nancy's car, write, "Buick."

Once the grid is completed and you understand what identity you've given each character, give blank grids to your students. After you've given a certain amount of basic information about a few grids, you can be as tricky with your descriptions as you like. For good classes, you can try "Susan is an accountant but Phil makes furniture." And later, "the carpenter [meaning Phil] lives in a townhouse." Students try to fill in all the grids with the characters' personal information.

After a few minutes of such description, you ask a deceptively easy question which is based on your long string of relationships such as "Who drives the Volvo?" Just make sure that all your relationships really have been tied together to create a "trail" leading to the answer.

*Map Game* (directions)--Two versions of a simple city map with street names and many shops and buildings are distributed to each pair of students. One version has half the shops identified, the other has the other half identified. Shops not identified are listed at the bottom of each page. Students face each other with a divider between them so the other map can't be seen.

Both students start from the same point on the map and take turns "leading" the partner to unidentified buildings by giving directions; e.g., "Now turn right on Elm St. and go up two blocks to the big tree. The pastry shop is behind the tree." First team to complete both maps wins.

_Drawing Game_ (shapes)--Discuss vocabulary of shapes: squares, rectangles, cubes, etc. Students are paired and each student is given one of two versions of a collection of five composite shapes; e.g., a square in a circle above a triangle. As in the _Map Game,_ students face each other with a divider between them. Each student must describe the shapes on his paper to his partner without gesturing until his partner thinks he's got it. After each student has described to his partner all five shapes, the class examines each team's efforts and names the most accurate reproductions as winners.

_Grid Games_ (directions, prepositions)--The _Drawing_ and _Map_ games obviously are similar in that students must describe what they see effectively enough for their team mate to approximate what is being described. Such games are often played on grids (pieces of paper, lined off into boxes) wherein players will arrange photos, drawings or even small objects, then describe that placement to their team mates so that an accurate description is possible.

A variation of this is to give the students two sets of objects and have them use their whole desk as a grid, placing objects in corners, on their sides, on top of one another, etc. In this case, its's probably wise to have students sit with their backs to each other, rather than relying on a simple paper divider between them.

_Debate_--Students are told to think of an individual living or dead whom they think is the most important person in the world. The students are then told that all their chosen people are passengers in a dropping balloon and all but one must jump out. Each student must defend for one minute why his choice should be the only person to survive. Students then vote for someone other than their own choice to decide the winner. (Of course, other scenarios such as a desert island, sinking boat, Arctic expedition, etc. are possible but the balloon may be the least "heavy." (Sorry again!))

*Interview*--Students are assigned three to a team and told to decide what famous person (living or dead) one of them would like to be. The other two team members act as interviewers of the celebrity. Allow about ten minutes for students to prepare their interview, then have them perform for the class. The class may vote on which celebrity they would like to have back for next week's show.

*Gossip* (reported speech)--Best if desks can be arranged in a circle but workable with conventional seating. The teacher works from a list of ten sentences demonstrating a recent teaching point; e.g., present progressive. One at a time, he whispers them to the first student who whispers them to the second, and so forth; e.g., "I'm eating a ripe red tomato. He's listening to an old Beatles record." A 30-second pause should be allowed between whispers to allow for "bottlenecks." The last student the whispers the utterance back to the teacher who notes what he hears next to what he originally said. Comparison of the two makes for pretty good hilarity.

*Bingo* (numbers; pronunciation)--Students should take turns calling the numbers, which should be quite large to exercise the Asian student's confusion with thousands and ten thousands (which, in Oriental languages, is a separate category between *thousand* and *million*). Also, rather than *b, i, n, g* and *o* being used, vary the row letters according to pronunciation needs: *f, s, b, v, e* (which students may pronounce "*a*"), *i* (which may come out "*e*"), *n, m,* etc. Although it may seem a little weird having students call out "V 13,000," they'll get more out of that kind of game than what we're used to at home. An alternative, of course, is just to pick up a kid's bingo game at a game store.

_Songs_ are an enjoyable classroom activity, especially among children or young adult students. Because the melody and lyrics are interwoven, retention of words seems heightened and certain structures can be very effectively presented in an entertaining way. You can almost always find someone in the class who plays the guitar and encourage him to bring it to class one day.

When selecting a song for class, be sure it has value in either grammar, pronunciation, vocabulary or culture. The tune should be simple and easily remembered. Lyrics should be repetitive with the chorus being especially easy to learn. Make sure the lyrics are standard English, not unusual slang or antiquated. Stick to conservative songs with simple messages--remember the song is for their language learning, not your nostalgia. If they're singing about how they "can't get no satisfaction," you could be inadvertently reinforcing bad grammar or worse, implying that grammar doesn't matter. There are plenty of good modern songs around that use good English.

When presenting a song, it's best to first introduce it by giving a bit of its history as well as background on who wrote it, then pass out copies of the lyrics or write them on the blackboard. (You might also consider leaving out a few words which the students will have to catch in the song.) Then sing or play the song through completely and read the lyrics out loud to the class, discussing any vocabulary or grammar points with them.

Have the class practice the chorus first, then the verses, one by one. Always model each verse yourself before asking the students to try it. Finally, sing the whole song through as a group several times and, if anyone in the class is an accomplished singer, invite him or her to give a solo performance.

Some traditional EFL songs include "Bingo" (teaches individual letter sounds), "Michael Row the Boat Ashore" (teaches the imperative, *l, r, s* and *h* sounds) "Oh Susanna" (simple past tense), "I've Been Working on the Railroad" (present perfect continuous tense and *can't*), "Red River Valley" (simple present, future and present tenses; modals *may* and *would;* sounds *l, r,* and *th)* and "The Drunken Sailor" (modal shall; sounds *l, r,* and *sh).* You'll find these and more in music store song books or at the library.

Pronunciation activities can be difficult due to pronunciation usually being practiced in isolation without any meaningful context. Especially for Japanese and Korean students with their "impoverished" systems of far fewer sounds than those commonly used in English, however, they are essential. There is nothing more frustrating (or common) for such students to have spent years learning English only to find on their first trip to the West that no one there can understand their accent.

In instruction, the teacher usually first models the correct sound, then explains in simple terms how the sound can be made and where the various speech organs are to be placed in the mouth. ("No, I'm not kidding. You really *do* need to put your tongue between your teeth.") The students then practice making the sound in isolation, in a word and with the word in a sentence. Individuals and the group as a whole try it with the teacher making corrections as needed.

It's best to teach pronunciation with "minimal pairs," that is, similar sounds which students frequently confuse. Such minimal pairs could be *b/v, th/s, p/b, d/g, z/d, sh/ch* or *l/r.* One popular minimal pair drill is having the teacher stand behind the students in the back of the class and say one of the minimal pair words which the students then have to guess by holding up one finger or two.

Students can then be paired off to see if their partner can guess which *they're* trying to say.

But rather than just having the students practice "*thick/sick*" a few dozen times, it's far better to try to contextualize the exercise by making either choice of the pair meaningful. One exercise to do this is to create two scenarios dependent on the minimal pair. For example, explain to the class the concept of "stealing a base." Then write on the board and teach them the phrase "He's stealing a base for his team." Next teach them "He's stealing a vase for his house." Write this on the board and have the students work with the different sounds.

Then move to the back of the room where the students can't see you and call the students to the front of the class one by one to face you. You then signal which sound you want the student to say (either *b* or *v)* by raising one finger or two. The student then says the appropriate opening phrase, "He's stealing a base" or "He's stealing a vase" and the students respond with the completion, "for his team" or "for his house." This gives meaning to the distinction between the sounds and makes the students realize just how subtle but important that difference can be.

(One of the most peculiar things I noticed when I began teaching was that not only can't many nationalities make certain sounds, they really can't *hear* them either. To many students, for example, *hit* and *heat* sound identical.)

<u>"Realia"</u> is becoming increasingly popular in the ESL/EFL classroom as teachers strive to bring more pieces of the real world into their language classes. By definition, "realia" can be any prop or artifact one would ordinarily encounter in the "real world."

Most language teachers tend to have the following as their basic "tool kit" although any item you encounter that you think would help illustrate your instruction should certainly be brought to class:

* a large calendar for teaching dates and tenses
* large maps or a globe to teach directions and country names
* crossword and picture puzzles
* a large clock with movable hands to teach time
* menus (many "chain" restaurants will supply you with a set of these before you go)
* tableware for dining etiquette instruction
* a collection of clothing
* post office materials
* magazine and newspapers for current events
* travel posters and brochures
* food packages
* a large paper thermometer for temperatures (Fahrenheit and Celsius)
* foreign money to practice giving and getting change
* mirrors for pronunciation instruction
* motor vehicle department booklets for sign and direction practice

If you'd like to invest a little money in "tools," you might want to purchase a "teletrainer" before you begin teaching. Basically, this device is just a set of two telephones with long cords and a control box which produces a ring or busy signal. The conversation on the line can be private or broadcast over a speaker to the whole class.

Students using the teletrainer should be placed so they can't see each other and use facial expressions or gestures.

Sometimes, your local phone company will give or loan a teletrainer to you. Otherwise, you can probably find one through a teaching supply company. If the expense is too great, you could take all the necessary ordering information to your boss and try to persuade him to buy one for the school.

A cheap alternative is get a simple intercom system, such as those sold by "Radio Shack" and other electronics stores.

Exercises with the teletrainer might include asking about store hours, when a film starts, product availability, making a business appointment, canceling an appointment and the ever-popular calling in late to work.

Teaching English in Asia is one of life's true joys, I believe. It's not very often that we have the opportunity to share something of ours with another human being who genuinely admires and values it. Such a gift is the English we give our students, probably the best motivated learners of our language on the planet. By organizing our teaching efforts, we can benefit them in a very real and meaningful way and, not incidentally, allow ourselves to experience their delightful countries which they seem to so enjoy sharing with us.

To be the best teacher possible in Asia's English classrooms, try to decide which method best suits your style and your students' needs. Bring some good non-text related materials with you to lend a little variety to your classes (especially games, pronunciation charts and "realia"). Familiarize yourself with the problems your students are likely to have, then decide how best to treat them.

Discourage translation, either spoken or in thought. Make your students respond quickly to your questions so they'll start thinking in English and not perform the usual "English question to native question to native thinking to native answer to English answer" process which can kill precious class time and probably drive you (and the other students) up the wall.

Keep your classes lively and laugh a lot. Studies have actually shown that humor is very beneficial in helping a student grasp a foreign language. Certainly it builds rapport and trust with the teacher.

You must honestly like your students and be curious about their lives. Encourage their efforts and emphasize to them how difficult their language is for you so they won't feel quite so discouraged when they make the same mistakes over and over.

Above all, have fun and enjoy your students' company. Try not to take on so many hours that students' faces all start to blur into a single mass of humanity before you. If you feel that happening, pull back--you're starting to burn out. If you pace yourself right and teach because you honestly want to share your language with people who sincerely want to learn it, you're guaranteed to have a thoroughly enjoyable and satisfying time teaching.

# Appendix

The following institutions offer post-graduate PhD, Master's degrees or Certificates in TEFL or TEFL-related areas. Some may also offer non-credit teacher-training programs for those not pursuing a graduate degree. For the purposes of teaching in Asia, a one-year Certificate program should provide adequate training.

*USA*

* Adelphi University, Institute for Teaching and Education Studies, Program in TESOL, Garden City NY 11530; tel. 516-663-1014. MA program.
* American University, Dept. of Language Studies, Program in Linguistics, Washington DC 20016; tel. 202-885-2394. MA and Certificate programs.
* Arizona State University, Dept. of English (TESL), Tempe AZ 85287; 602-965-3168. MA program.
* Azusa Pacific University, College of Arts and Sciences. TESL Program, Azusa CA 91702; tel. 818-969-3434, ext. 3555. MA and Certificate programs.
* Azusa Pacific University, Dept. of Education, Azusa CA 91702; tel. 818-969-3434, ext. 3075. MEd in TESL program.
* Boston University, School of Education, TESOL Program, Boston MA 02215; tel. 617-353-3233. MEd in TESL.

* Bowling Green State University, Dept. of English (TESL), Bowling Green OH 43403; tel. 419-372-2576. MA TESL.

* Brigham Young University, Dept. of Linguistics, Provo UT 84602; tel. 801-378-2937. MA and Certificate programs.

* California State University, Dept. of Graduate Education (TESL), Carson CA 90747; tel. 213-516-3522. Certificate program.

* California State University, Department of English (TESL), Carson CA 90747; tel. 213-516-3322. Certificate program.

* California State University, Department of Linguistics (TESL), Fresno CA 93740; tel. 209-294-2441. MA program.

* California State University, Dept. of Foreign Languages (TESOL), Fullerton CA 92634; tel. 714-773-3534. MS in TESOL.

* California State University, Dept. of English (TESL), Sacramento CA 95819; tel. 916-278-6247. MA in TESOL.

* Central Missouri State University, Dept. of English (TESL), Warrensburg MO 64093; tel. 816-429-4426. MA.

* Central Washington University, Dept. of English (TESL), Ellensburg WA 98926; tel. 509-963-1546. MA in TESL, MA in TEFL.

* College of New Rochelle, Dept. of Education (TESL), New Rochelle NY 10805; tel. 914-654-5330. MSEd in TESL.

* Columbia Bible College, Graduate School of Missions (TESL), Columbia SC 29230; tel. 803-754-4100.

* Eastern Michigan University, Dept. of Foreign Languages (TESOL), Ypsilanti MI 48197; tel. 313-487-0433. MA in TESOL.

* George Mason University, Dept. of English (TESL), Fairfax VA 22030; tel. 703-323-2698. Certificate in TESL.

* Georgia State University, College of Public Affairs (TESL), Atlanta GA 30303; tel. 404-651-2584. MS in TESL.

* Georgia State University, College of Education (TESL), Atlanta GA 30303; tel. 404-651-2584. MEd in TESL.
* Holy Names College, Dept. of Education (TESL), Oakland CA 94619; tel. 415-436-1064. Certificate.
* Hunter College, CUNY, Division of Education, Dept. of Teaching (TESL), New York, NY 10021; tel. 212-772-4691. MA in TESL.
* Indiana University, Dept. of English (TESL), Indiana PA 15705; tel. 412-357-2261. MA and PhD in TEFL/TESL.
* Inter-American University, Dept. of English, San German, Puerto Rico 00753; tel. 809-892-1095 ext. 311. MA in TESL.
* Jersey City State College, Bilingual Education Program. Jersey City, NJ 07305; tel. 201-547-3374. MA in TESL.
* Long Island University, School of Education (TESOL), Brooklyn NY 11201; tel. 718-403-1055. MSEd in TESL.
* Long Island University, Faculty of Education, Dept. of Instruction (TESL), Brookville NY 11548; tel. 516-299-2372. MS in TESL.
* Maryville College, Education Division (TESL), St. Louis MO 63141; tel. 314-576-9472. MA in TESL.
* Michigan State University, Dept. of English (TESL), East Lansing, MI 48824; tel. 517-355-7570. MA in TESOL.
* Monterey Institute of International Studies, Program in TESOL Monterey CA 93940; tel. 408-647-4182.
* Nazareth College, Graduate Program in Education (TESOL), Rochester NY 14610. MSEd in TESOL.
* New York University, Division of Education. Dept. of Communication Arts (TESOL), New York, NY 10011; tel. 212-998-5235. MA in TESL.
* Northeastern Illinois University, Dept. of Linguistics (TESL), Chicago IL 60625; tel. 312-583-4050. MA in TESL.

* Notre Dame College, Dept. of Education (TESL), Manchester NH 03104; tel. 603-669-4298. MEd in TESL.
* Oral Roberts University, School of Education (TESL), Tulsa OK 74171; tel. 918-495-6004. MA Ed in TESL.
* Pan American University, Dept. of English (TESL), Edinburg TX 78539; tel. 512-381-3421. MA in TESL.
* Pennsylvania State University, Dept. of Speech (TESL), University Park PA 16802; tel. 814-865-3461. MA in TESL.
* Portland State University (TESOL), Dept. of English, Portland OR 97207; tel. 503-464-4088. MA in TESOL.
* Queens College of CUNY, Dept. of Linguistics (TESL), Flushing NY 11367; tel. 718-520-7161. MSEd in TESL.
* Rhode Island College, Dept. of Secondary Education (TESL), Providence RI 02908; tel. 401-456-8018. MEd in TESL.
* Rutgers University, Dept. of Learning and Teaching (TESL), New Brunswick NJ 08903; tel. 201-932-7938. MEd in TESL.
* Saint Michael's College, TESL Program, Winooski VT 05404; tel. 802-655-2000 ext. 2300. MA in TESL.
* San Jose State University, Dept of Linguistics (TESL), San Jose CA 95192; tel. 408-924-4483. MA in TESL.
* School for International Training, TESL Program, Brattleboro VT 05301; tel. 802-257-7751. MA in TESL.
* Seton Hall University, Teacher Training Program (TESL), South Orange NJ 07079; tel. 201-761-9395. MA in TESL.
* Southern Illinois University, Dept. of Linguistics (TESL), Carbondale IL 62901; tel. 618-536-3385. MA in TESL.
* State University of New York, Dept. of Learning and Instruction (TESL), Buffalo NY 14260; tel. 716-636-2455. MA in TESL.

* State University of New York, Dept. of Linguistics (TESL), Stony Brook, NY 11794; tel. 516-632-7775. MA in TESL.
* State University of New York, Dept. of Education (TESL), Brockport NY 14420; tel. 716-395-5554. MSEd in TESL.
* Syracuse University, School of Education (TESL), Syracuse NY 13244; tel. 315-443-4757. MS in TESL.
* Teachers College, Dept. of Languages (TESOL), New York NY 10027; tel. 212-678-3710. MEd and MA in TESOL.
* University of Alabama, Dept. of English (TESL), Tuscaloosa AL 35487; tel. 205-348-5065. MA in TESL.
* University of Arizona, Dept. of English (TESL), Tucson AZ 85721; tel. 602-621-1358. MA in TESL.
* University of California, Dept. of English (TESOL), Los Angeles CA 90024; tel. 213-825-4632.
* University of Hawaii, Dept. of English (ESL), Honolulu HI 96822. MA in TESL.
* University of Idaho, Dept. of English (TESL), Moscow ID 83843; tel. 208-885-6156. MA in TESL.
* University of Illinois, English as an International Language (TESOL), Urbana IL 61801; tel. 217-333-1506. MA in TESL.
* University of Kansas, School of Education (TESL), Lawrence KS 66045. MA and MSEd in TESL.
* University of Massachusetts, College of Arts and Sciences (TESOL), Boston MA 02125; tel. 617-929-8300. MA in TESL.
* University of Northern Iowa, Dept. of English (TESL), Cedar Falls IA 50614; tel. 319-273-2821. MA in TESL.
* University of Northern Iowa, Dept. of Modern Languages (TESL), Cedar Falls IA 50614; tel. 319-273-2749. MA in TESL.
* University of North Texas, Dept. of English (TESL), Denton TX 76203; tel. 817-565-2050. MA in TESL.

* University of Pennsylvania, Language in Education (TESOL), Philadelphia PA 19104; tel. 215-898-7913. MSEd in TESOL.
* University of San Francisco, School of Education (TESL), San Francisco CA 94117. MA in TESL.
* University of South Carolina, Program in Linguistics (TESL), Columbia SC 29208; tel. 803-777-2063. Certificate in TESL.
* University of South Florida, Program in Applied Linguistics (TESL), Tampa FL 33620; tel. 813-974-2517. MA in TESL.
* University of Texas, Dept. of Foreign Language Education (TESL), Austin TX 78713; tel. 512-471-4078. MA in TESL.
* University of Texas, Division of Bilingual Studies (TESL), San Antonio TX 78285; tel. 512-691-4426. MA in TESL.
* Utah State University, Dept. of English (TESL), Logan UT 84322; tel. 801-750-2743. MA in TESL.
* Wayne State University, Division of Teacher Education (TESL), Detroit MI 48202; tel. 313-577-0922. EdS and MEd in TESL.
* West Chester University, Dept. of English (TESL), West Chester PA 19383. MA in TESL.
* Western Michigan University, Dept. of Education (TESL), Kalamazoo MI 49008; tel. 616-387-3465. MA in TESL.
* West Virginia University, Program in Linguistics (TESOL), Morgantown WV 26506; tel. 304-293-5121. MA in TESOL.
* Wright State University, Dept. of English Language (TESOL), Dayton OH 45435; tel. 513-873-3136. MA in TESOL.
* Concordia University, Center for TESL, Montreal PQ H3G 1M8 CANADA; tel. 514-848-2446. MA in Applied Linguistics.
* McGill University, Dept. of Education in Second Languages, Montreal PQ H3A 2T5 CANADA; tel. 514-398-6982. MEd in TESL.

## SELECTED REFERENCE BOOKS

* Celce-Murcia, Marianne; <u>Teaching English as a Second or Foreign Language</u>; Newbury House.

* Claire, Elizabeth; <u>ESL Teachers' Holiday Activities Kit;</u> P-H.

* Clark, Raymond; <u>Index Card Games for ESL;</u> Pro Lingua.

* Davis, Dee; <u>Real Life Spoken English;</u> Spoken English Pub.

* Dennis, John, <u>English Through Drama;</u> Alemany Pr.

* Dixson, Robert; <u>Practical Guide to Teaching English as a Foreign Language</u>; Prentice ESL.

* Elbaum, Sandra; <u>Tell Me More;</u> Scott F.

* <u>Elementary English for Koreans;</u> IBD Ltd.

* Esarey, Gary; <u>Pronunciation Exercises...;</u> U of Mich Pr.

* Evans, Norman; <u>Beyond Words;</u> P-H.

* Hines, Mary; <u>Skits in English;</u> Prentice ESL.

* Hjelt, M. Christine; <u>Teaching English... (Volunteer);</u> NAFSA Washington.

* Ilyin, Donna; <u>Classroom Practices in Adult ESL;</u> Tchrs Eng Spkrs.

* Jerald, Michael; <u>Experiential Language Teaching Techniques;</u> Pro Lingua.

* Keyes, Joan; <u>Now You're Talking</u>; Ed Activities.

* Kimizuka, Sumako; <u>Teaching English to Japanese</u>; Neptune Books.

* Kirn, Elaine; <u>ESL Grammar</u>; McGraw.

* Larsen-Freeman, Diane; <u>Techniques and Principles in Language Teaching</u>; Oxford U Pr.

* Lewis, Michael; <u>Source Book for Teaching English Overseas</u>; Heinemann Ed.

* McCallum, George; <u>Brief Encounters (Practice and Activities)</u>; Harper Collins.

* Rivers, Wilga; <u>Communicating Naturally in a Second Language</u>; Cambridge U Pr.

* Robinson, Barbara; <u>Focus: An ESL Grammar</u>; St. Martins.

* Taylor, Grant; <u>English Conversation Practice</u>; McGraw.

* Terry, John R; <u>Cultural Gaps: East & West</u>; Dawn Pr.

* Walpole, Hugh; <u>Foundations of English for Foreign Students</u>; Bks Demand UMI.

* Welmers, William; <u>Spoken English as a Foreign Language</u>; Spoken Language Service.

* Wennerstrom, Ann; <u>Techniques for Teachers</u>; U of Mich Pr.

* Wharton, John; <u>JOBS IN JAPAN--The Complete Guide to Living and Working in the Land of Rising Opportunity</u>; Global Press.

## VISA AND TOURIST INFORMATION

Most countries have only one embassy in the foreign country's capital and several consulates in that country's major cities. In most cases, foreigners are asked to contact the nearest office but, in the case of some special information (e.g., the JET Program or economic or business affairs), one should contact the embassy directly.

Because the Republic of China (Taiwan) has no formal diplomatic relations with most Western countries, various quasi-governmental organizations have been established. The nearest Coordination Council for North American Affairs (CCNAA) office (or equivalent for non-Americans) is the appropriate contact for all foreigners seeking such assistance.

Although most countries' tourist information offices are, of course, intended to assist foreign tourists part with as much of their money as possible, the Japan National Tourist Organization (JNTO), the Korea National Tourism Corporation (KNTC) or Taiwan's CCNAA, can be a good source of general information and especially maps for those intending to live and work in the country as well .

*JAPAN*

&ast; Japanese Embasssy, 2520 Massachusetts Ave. NW; Washington DC 20008; tel. 202-234-2266.

&ast; Japanese Consulate, 50 Fremont St., San Francisco CA 94105; tel. 415-777-3533.

&ast; Japanese Consulate, 250 E. 1st St. #1507, Los Angeles CA 90012; tel. 213-624-8305.

&ast; Japanese Consulate, 299 Park Ave., NYC NY 10171; tel. 212-371-8222.

&ast; Embassy of Japan, 255 Sussex Dr., Ottawa K1N 9E6; tel. 613-236-8541.

&ast; Embassy of Japan, 101-104 Piccadilly, London W1V 9FN; tel. 01-465-6500.

&ast; JNTO, 360 Post St #401, San Francisco CA 94108; tel. 415-989-7140.

* JNTO, 630 Fifth Ave., NYC NY 10111; tel. 212-757-5640.

* JNTO, 165 University Ave., Toronto M5H 3B8; tel. 416- 366-7140.

* JNTO 167 Regent St., London W1; tel. 071-734-9638.

*KOREA*

* Korean Embassy, 2370 Massachusetts Ave. NW, Washington DC; tel. 202-939-5662.

* Korean Consulate, 3243 Wilshire Blvd., Los Angeles CA 90010; tel. 213-385-9300.

* Korean Consulate, 3500 Clay St., San Francisco CA 94118; tel. 415-921-2251/3.

* Korean Consulate; 2033 6th Ave. #1125, Seattle WA 98121; tel. 206-441-1011/4.

* Korean Consulate, 460 Park Ave. 5F, NYC NY 10022; tel. 212-752-1700.

* Korean Consulate, 439 University Ave. #700, Toronto, Ontario M5G 1Y8; tel. 416-598-4608/9.

* Korean Consulate, 830-1066 West Hastings St., Vancouver BC V6E 3X1; tel. 604-681-9581.

* Korean Embassy, 4 Palace Gate, London UK W8 5NF; tel. 01-581-0247/9/0.

* Korean Embassy, Elders House 86-94 6F, Victoria St., Wellington, New Zealand; tel. 04-739-073/4.

* Korean Consulate, 32-36 Martin Place 8F, Sydney, NSW; tel. 02-221-3806/3697.

* KNTC, 3435 Wilshire Blvd. #350, Los Angeles CA 90010; tel. 213-382-3435.

* KNTC, 2 Executive Dr. 7F, Ft. Lee NJ 07024; tel. 201-585-0909.

* KNTC, 480 University Ave. #406, Toronto, Ont. M5G 1V2; tel. 416-348-9056.

* KNTC, Vogue House 2F, 1 Hanover Sq., London W1R 9RD; tel. 01-409-2100.

## TAIWAN

* CCNAA, 801 2nd Ave. 6F, New York NY 10017; tel. 212-370-6600.
* CCNAA Travel Section, 1 WTC #7953, New York, NY 10048; tel. 212-466-0691/2.
* CCNAA, 555 Montgomery St. #501, San Francisco CA 94111; tel. 415-362-7680.
* CCNAA Travel Section, 166 Geary St. San Francisco CA 94108; tel. 415-989-8677.
* CCNAA, 4201 Wisconsin Ave. NW, Washington DC 20016; tel. 202-895-1800.
* CCNAA, 2 Midtown Plaza #1290, 1349 W. Peachtree St. NE, Atlanta GA 30309, Tel. 404-872-0123.
* CCNAA, 99 Summer St. #801, Boston MA 02110; tel. 617- 737-2050.
* CCNAA, 20 N. Clark St., 19F, Chicago IL 60602; tel. 312-372-1213/4.
* CCNAA, 2746 Pali Hwy., Honolulu HI 96817; tel. 808-595-3462.
* CCNAA, 11 Greenway Plaza #2006, Houston TX 77046; tel. 713-626-7445/7.
* CCNAA, 3100 Broadway #1001, Kansas City MO 64111; tel. 816-531-1298.
* CCNAA, 3660 Wilshire Blvd #918, Los Angeles CA 90010; tel. 213-380-3644.
* CCNAA, 2333 Ponce de Leon Blvd. #610, Coral Gables FL 33134.
* CCNAA, 2001 6th Ave. 24F, Seattle WA 98121; tel. 206-441-4586.

* Chung-Hwa (CCNAA), 123 Edward St., Toronto M5G 1E2; tel. 416-977-5744/62.
* Free Chinese Centre, 14-16 Regent St., London SW1Y 4PH; tel., 071-930-5767.
* Chinese Trade and Culture Center, 10-11 S. Leinster St., Dublin, Ireland; tel. 785413.
* Far East Trading Co., MLC Center, Martin Place #1904, Sydney NSW 2000 Australia; tel. 02-231-6942.

## LOW-COST ACCOMMODATIONS IN KOREA

For cheap, clean and culturally-authentic accommodations, the *yogwan* is highly recommended. In this Korean-style inn, guests sleep on a matress placed on a heated floor. Prices range from 12,000 to 25,000 won with the widest assortment to be found in Seoul behind the City Hall and Sejong Cultural Center.

For clean and comfortable shared accommodations, try hostels which welcome guests of any age as long as they are members of the International Youth Hostel Association (memberships available in Seoul). Hostel prices range from 6,000 to 9,000 won, giving members a room often identical to a standard hotel room but with as many as eight people sharing. Good fun and a great way to pick up job information!

### YOGWANS

*SEOUL*

* Daewon Yogwan/Inn Daewon, Dangju-dong, Chon gno-gu; tel. 735-7891.
* Sung Do Yogwan, 120 Naesu-dong; tel. 738-8226.
* Kwang Pyung Yogwan, 123-1 Ta-dong; tel. 778-0104.

### YOUTH HOSTELS

*SEOUL*

* Bando YH, 679-3 Yoksam-dong, Kangnam-ku; tel. 567-3111/5.
* Olympic YH, 88 Pang-i-dong, Songp'a-gu; 410-2114.
* Seoul ECC YH, 202, Yagjae-dong, Soch'o-gu; 751-8100.

*PUSAN*

 * Aerin YH, 41-1-ga, Posu-dong, Chung-gu; tel. 257- 2222/7.
 * Kum Gang YH, 1-4 Onch'on-dong, Tongnae-gu; 554-3235/9.

*KYONGGI PROVINCE*

 * Jaeil YH, San 581, Pugok-dong, Ansan; tel. 80-4111/3.
 * Koyang YH, 278, Koyang-ri, Pyokche-up, Koyang-gun; tel. 62-9049.
 * Bulam YH, Hwajop-ri, Pyoilae-myon, Namyangju-gun; tel. 0346-65-8081.

*KANGWON PROVINCE*

 * Naksan YH, 30-1, Chonjin-ri, Kanghyon-myon, Yayangyang-gun; tel. 0396-672-3416/8.
 * Sorak YH, 155, Tomun-dong, Sokcho; tel. 0392-34-7540/50 or 02-763-9871 (Seoul telephone).

## LOW-COST ACCOMMODATIONS IN TAIWAN

The following hostels in Taipei offer air conditioned rooms, showers, kitchen and laundry facilities for between NT$160 and $250 per night. All feature dorm-style rooms while some offer single and twin rooms also . As anywhere, hostels in Taiwan are a great place to pick up the latest information and make interesting friends.

* ABC Hostel, 14F-3, 266 Fu Hising N. Rd.; tel. 507- 3397
* Amigo Hostel, 4F 286 Chi Lin Rd.; tel. 542-0292.
* Formosa Hostel, 3F, 16, Lane 20, Chungshan N. Rd, Sec. 2; tel. 562-2035.
* Friendly House, 10F, 50 Po Ai Rd.; tel. 381-8804.
* Happy Family Hostel, 4F, 16-1 Pei Ping W. Rd; tel. 375-3443.
* Keyman's Inn, 1 Hwaining St.; tel. 311-4811.
* Namaste Hostel, 3F 85 Chunghsiao W. Rd., Sec. 1; tel. 331-6427.
* Rainbow Hostel, 91 Chungshan N. Rd., Sec. 3; tel. 596-5515.
* Roosevelt Hostel, 4F, 96-5 Hsin Sheng S. Rd., Sec. 3; tel. 363-8943.
* Sweet Home Hostel, 12 Alley 3, Lane 329, Wamta Rd.; tel. 307-6853.
* Taipei Hostel, 6F, 11 Lane 5, Lin Sen N. Rd.; tel. 395- 2950.
* Yang Min Shen Hostel, 12 Yang Min Rd.; tel. 861-6601.
* YMCA, 19 Hsu Chang St.; tel. 311-3201.

## CHINESE LANGUAGE SCHOOLS

Many Westerners living in Taiwan are full-time students of Mandarin Chinese studying a minimum of ten hours per week. Enrollment in such a program often serves as justification to remain in that country for a total of six months whereupon a new visitor's visa may be necessary.

* California State University International Program, 187 Chinhua St., Taipei; tel. 391-2417.
* Cathay Chinese Language Center, 8, Lane 190 Chung Shan N. Rd., Sec. 7, Taipei; tel. 872-9165.
* China Language Institute, 4, Lane 82 Anho Rd., Taipei; tel. 708-7157. Also 51 Tienmou N. Rd., Taipei; tel. 872-7127. Also teaches English to Chinese.
* Everyday Language Center (ELC), 72 Chunghsiao W. Rd., Sec. 1, Taipei; tel. 311-4595.
* Inter-University Program, Stanford University, PO Box 13-204, Taipei; tel. 363-9123.
* International Chinese Institute (ICI), Rm. 418, 41 Chunghsiao W. Rd., Sec. 1, Taipei; tel., 371-8277.
* Jordan's Language School, 97 Chuan Gow St.; tel. 309-0863.
* Lancer Language School, 1 Lane 62 Alley 10, Chih Cheng Rd. Sec. 1, Shih Lin; tel. 835-5451.
* Language Training & Testing Center, 170 Hsinhai Rd., Sec. 2, Taipei; tel. 362-6385.
* Mandarin Daily News, 10 Fu Chow St.; tel. 391-5134.
* MY Language School, 126-8 Singsheng S. Rd. Sec. 1, Taipei; tel. 321-7636. Also teaches English.
* Shi-da (National Normal) University, 129-1 Hoping East Rd., Sec. 1; tel. 321-8457.
* Taipei Language Institute, 104 Hsin Yi Rd., Sec. 2, Taipei; tel. 393-8805.
* Taipei Language Institute, 238 Shih Tung Rd., Shih Lin, Taipei; tel. 832-7330.
* Taipei Language Institute, 16 Lane 118, Chin Hua N. Rd., Taichung; tel. 04-231-8842. Also 37 Chung Hua 3rd Road, Kaohsiung; tel. 07-251-3638.

## SUGGESTED CLASSROOM NAMES

The following names have been chosen as appropriate for classroom use because each has within it some pronunciation problem for the Asian student. Encourage correct pronunciation always.

### MEN:

Aaron, Abel, Abner, Abraham, Adrian , Alan, Albert, Alexander, Alexander, Alfred, Andrew, Anthony, Arnold , Arthur, Barry, Bernard, Bert, Bill, Brett, Brian, Broderick, Bruce, Byron, Calvin, Cameron, Carey, Carl, Charles, Christopher, Clifford, Colin, Corey, Craig, Curtis , Dale, Daniel, Darrell, David, Dennis, Derrick, Donald, Douglas, Edgar, Edward, Eric, Ernest, Erwin, Frank, Gabriel, Gerald, Glenn, Gordon, Gregory, Harold, Harry, Herbert, Jeffrey, Lawrence, Lloyd, Mark, Marshall, Mitchell, Murray, Patrick, Perry, Ralph, Randolph, Roland, Ronald, Rudolph, Samuel, Theodore, Tracy, Vernon, Victor, Vincent, Virgil, Walter, Walton, Warner, Wilbur, William.

### WOMEN:

Abigail, Alice, Andrea, Angelica, Annabelle, April, Arlene, Audrey , Aurora, Barbara, Beth, Beverly, Blythe, Brenda, Camille, Cara, Carla, Carol, Caroline, Cathleen, Celeste, Charlotte, Clara, Claudia, Crystal, Cynthia, Darlene, Deborah, Delilah, Dolores, Doris, Dorothy, Edith, Eleanor, Elizabeth, Ella, Emily, Erma, Estelle, Esther, Evangeline, Evelyn, Faith, Fern, Florence, Frances, Gail, Gladys, Gloria, Harriet, Heather, Irene, Judith, Kelly, Kimberly, Laraine, Laura, Lena, Leslie, Lillian, Lynn, Martha, Melissa, Miriam, Muriel, Myrna, Norma, Ophelia, Pamela, Paula, Phyllis, Priscilla, Rachel, Ruth, Samantha, Scarlett, Sheila, Shirley, Tabitha, Thelma, Valerie, Verna, Veronica, Victoria, Virginia, Vivian, Wilhemina.

## ENGLISH SCHOOLS IN JAPAN

The following private English schools in Japan all employ native speakers as English instructors and usually are in need of such teachers, especially before semesters begin in September and April. The list is alphabetical and includes schools in every major city in Japan.

Mention in this directory is no assurance of quality. It's advisable to ask current employees (especially foreign teachers) about conditions at the school before making any type of commitment.

TOKYO SCHOOLS *("03" dialing area)*

* ABC; Tokyo, Chuo-ku, Nihonbashi, Murofuji Goe Bldg.; tel. 3242-7261.
* Academia; Tokyo, Shibuya-ku, Tomigaya 1-35; tel. 3465-8939.
* Access, Teisen Kandabashi Bldg. 5F, 1-27 Nishiki, Kanda, Tokyo; tel. 3291-6751.
* Albion Gakuin; 167, Tokyo, Suginami-ku, Showan 3-26-24; tel. 3333-9081. Four foreign teachers.
* Alec Gaigo Gakuin; 150, Tokyo, Shibuya 1-14-13 Daini Kobayashi Bldg. 5F; tel. 3400-4515. Nine foreign teachers.
* Alf English School; Tokyo, Adachi-ku, Nishi Arai 2-18; tel. 3896-0460.
* Alfa English School; Tokyo, Shibuya, Komatsu Bldg.; ; tel. 3486-8185.
* Alfa English School; Tokyo, Shibuya, Aoyama Laurel Bldg.; tel. 3498-2462.
* Alpha English School, 4-7 Shimo Ishigami, Tokyo; tel. 3904-3424.
* American Academy; Tokyo, Shinagawa-ku, Nishi Gotanda 2-24; tel. 3495-0881.
* American Family Club; Tokyo, Shibuya-ku, Minami Hiradai 12; tel. 3476-2241.

\* American House Eikaiwa Center; 188, Tokyo, Tanashi-shi, Hommachi 5-4-1; tel. 0424-64-0930. Three foreign teachers.

\* American Radio; Tokyo, Chiyoda-ku, Misaki, Misaki-cho, Florence Bldg.; tel. 3265-5705.

\* Anglo World; Tokyo; tel. 3648-6881.

\* Anglo-Continental Educational Group, 3-15 Roppongi, Minato-ku, Tokyo; tel. 3582-9735.

\* Ann's American Conversation Kyoshitsu, 2-19 Takadanobaba, Shinjuku-ku, Tokyo; tel. 3205-2425.

\* Aoki Shigeru; Tokyo, Adachi-ku, Adachi 4-30; tel. 3 887-0768.

\* Aoyama English School; Tokyo, Minato-ku, Minami-Aoyama 2-2; tel. 3405-5563.

\* ASA; 160, Tokyo, Shinjuku-ku, Nishi-Shinjuku 1-19-6, Yamate Shinjukku Bldg.; tel. 3348-3333. 150 foreign teachers, selective hiring.

\* Asahi Culture Center; 160, Tokyo, Nishi-Shinjuku, 2-6-1 1, Sumitomo Bldg.; tel. 3344-1941. Unlikely to sponsor but employs 22 foreign teachers.

\* Asia Center/PARC; 101, Tokyo, Chiyoda-ku, Kanda, Jimbocho 1-30, Seiko Bldg. 4F; tel. 3291-5901. All foreign teachers (3).

\* Athenee Francais; 101, Tokyo, Chiyoda-ku, Kanda, 2-11 Surugadai; tel. 3291-3391. Teaches many languages. 25 foreign teachers.

\* Azabu Academy; 106, Tokyo, Roppongi 3-14-12, Shuwa Roppongi Bldg. #701; tel. 3404-2841. Accelerated courses. All foreign teachers (8).

\* Baberu Honyaku Gakuin, NS Bldg. 2-2-3 Sarugaku-cho, Chiyoda-ku, Tokyo 101; tel. 3295-5155. 2 foreign teachers.

\* Barcino School; Tokyo, Shibuya-ku, Dogenzaka 1-15; tel. 3496-5955.

\* BEC; 160, Tokyo, Shinjuku 3-28-10; tel. 3352-2958. Large school with 73 foreign teachers.

\* Berkeley House Center, Topure Bldg. 4-2, Gobancho, Chiyoda-ku, Tokyo 102; tel. 3262-2711. TESL background, North American only.

\* Berlitz School, Asia Bldg., Kami Minami, Shibuya-ku, Tokyo; tel. 3461-5201.

* Berlitz School, Daini Koa Bldg. 1-11-39 Akasaka, Minato-ku, Tokyo 107; tel. 3584-4211. World-wide chain. 190 foreign teachers.

* Berlitz; Tokyo, Chuo-ku, Nihonbashi, Sanken Muromachi Bldg.; tel. 3243-0381.

* Berlitz; Tokyo, Chuo-ku, Nihonbashi, Dick Bldg.; tel. 3274-6701.

* Berlitz; Tokyo, Meguro-ku, Jiyugaoka, Obara Bldg.; tel. 3724-3781.

* Berlitz; Tokyo, Minato-ku, Kita Aoyama 3-3; tel. 3423-0361.

* Berlitz; Tokyo, Nishi Shinjuku, Daini Takakura Bldg.; tel. 3342-4751.

* Berlitz; Tokyo, Toyoshima-ku, Higashi Ikebukuro, Soba Bldg.; tel. 3983-6221.

* Best; Tokyo, Yotsuya 3-chome, Fudosan Kaikan 503; tel. 3351-4191.

* Bilingual Tokyo; 150, Tokyo, Shibuya-ku, Utagawa-cho 39-2, Village 80 Bldg. 4F; tel. 3477-1858. Large school with 170 foreign teachers.

* Bougnan English School; Toyoshima-ku, Higashi Ikebukuro 1-25-3; tel. 3983-7151. Features Business English.

* Bravis School of Languages, Taisei Bldg., 1-1-18 Akasaka, Tokyo; tel. 3586-1828.

* Bridge Center; Tokyo, Chuo-ku, Kyobashi, Irifune Honkan Bldg.; tel. 3281-4066.

* Brittania Gaigo Gakuin; 120, Tokyo, Adachi-ku, Ayase 3-3-1, Hoshi Bldg. 3F; tel. 3629-8681. All British teachers (18).

* Bunka Language Center; Tokyo, Shibuya-ku, Yoyogi 3-22; tel. 3370-3111.

* Bunsai Kenkyujo; Tokyo, Shinjuku-ku, Takadanobaba, Chiyoda Seimei Bldg.; tel. 3209-4971.

* Business Heights English Conversation School, 5-67 Nakano, Nakano-ku, Tokyo; tel. 3388-3227.

* BUV; Tokyo, Suginami-ku, Shimo Ibusan, Nakae Bldg.; tel. 3397-5609.

* Buzz International; Tokyo, Minato-ku, Roppongi 7-18; tel. 3402-9863.

* Cambridge Academy; Tokyo, Shibuya-ku, Udogawa 2; tel. 3462-2613.
* Cambridge English School; 160, Tokyo, Nishi-Shinjuku 1-13-12, Showa Bldg.; tel. 3348-0181. Teachers must have RSA credential (British).
* CCC, 1-15 Jingumae, Shibuya-ku, Tokyo; tel. 3404-6888.
* Century Eigo Gakuin; 105, Tokyo, Minato-ku, Hammamatsu-cho 1-25-3; tel. 3434-9484. 6 foreign teachers.
* Century Language School; Tokyo, Minato-ku, Hamamatsu Watanabe Bldg.; tel. 3434-7484.
* Children Eigo Gakuin, 1-23 Toshima, Kita-ku, Tokyo; tel. 3912-8526.
* Children English School; Tokyo, Nerima-ku, Fujimidai 2-4; tel. 3990-0664.
* Chuo Eigo Gakuin, 2-23 Nakano, Nakano-ku, Tokyo; tel. 3382-2098.
* Chuo Steno College; 160, Tokyo, Nishi-Shinjuku 7-4-7, Ota Bldg.; tel. 3362-4191. 4 foreign teachers.
* CIC; Tokyo, Minato-ku, Kita Aoyama 3-5; tel. 3475-0261.
* CLC; 103, Tokyo, Chuo-ku, Yaesu 1-9-13, Yaesu Ekimae Godo Bldg. 5F; tel. 3275-0151. All foreign teachers (20). ✓
* Clover English Center; Tokyo, Kita-ku, Akabane, Sanyo Bldg.; tel. 3903-3611.
* Comet Eikaiwa School, Sakata Bldg. 2F, 1-16-14 Hyakunin-cho, Shinjuku-ku, Tokyo; tel. 3362-3909.
* Comet International; Tokyo, Shinagawa-ku, Kamiozaki 4-5; tel. 3494-7166.
* Conan Gaigo School; 102, Tokyo, Chiyoda-ku, Ichiban-cho 4, Sagamiya Bldg.; tel. 3234-3358. 6 foreign teachers.
* Conan Language School; Tokyo, Shibuya-ku, Engaku Miura Bldg.; tel. 3463-9712.
* The Concord School of English, Kuroda Heights, 6-6-16 Akasaka, Minato-ku, Tokyo; tel. 3585-1084.

* Cosmo Language Center; Tokyo, Minato-ku, Akasaka, Kaneharu Bldg.; tel. 3582-0561.
* Cosmopolitan Language Institute, Yaesu B Bldg., Yaesu 1-8-9, Chuo-ku, Tokyo 103; tel. 3273-7878. Classes from 8 a.m. to 9 p.m. Principly for businessmen.
* Cosmopolitan; Tokyo, Toyoshima-ku, Nishi Ikebukuro 1-29; tel. 3988-8317.
* Create English School; Tokyo, Shinjuku 4-2; tel. 3 354-4601.
* Cross Continental, SK Bldg., Miyamasuzaka 14-8, Shibuya-ku, Tokyo 150 tel. 3409-0051.
* Deck's International School, Fujio Bldg. 2F & 3F, 3-49-3 Chuo, Nakano-ku, Tokyo; tel. 3367-5032.
* Don Bosco English Conversation Club, 3-11 Arakawa, Tokyo; tel. 3801-8296.
* East West English Center, Sanno Grand Bldg., Nagatacho, Chiyoda-ku, Tokyo; tel. 3581-7571.
* ECC; 160, Tokyo, Shinjuku-ku, Kabuki-cho 1-5-4, Dairoku Arai Bldg.; tel. 3209-3733. Very large chain. 44 schools and 200 foreign teachers. All types of English.
* ECC; Tokyo, Chiyoda-ku, Uchikanda, Daini Tomoe Bldg.; tel. 3256-1703.
* ECC; Tokyo, Nishi Ikebukuro, Chitoku Bldg.; tel. 3989-0531.
* ECS, Sogo Dairoku Bldg., 12-4 Hirakawa-cho 1-chome, Chiyoda-ku, Tokyo; tel. 3230-3286.
* Edward English Conversation School, 3-38 Soshigaya, Setagaya-ku, Tokyo; tel. 3482-2250.
* Eifel School; Shinjuku-ku, Shimoochiai, Nihon Tsuyaku Kyokai Bldg.; tel. 3367-0615.
* Eigo Gakuin; 164, Tokyo, Nakano-ku, Nakano 2-23-1; tel. 3380-6970. 2 foreign teachers.
* Eigo Semmon Kenkyujo; 110, Tokyo, Higashi Ueno 6-2-2, Maruyoshi Bldg.; tel. 3844-3104. 2 foreign teachers.
* Eikaiwa Gakuin; 185, Kunitachi-shi, Higashi 1-6, Hoshino Bldg.; tel. 0425-72-3719. All American teachers (13).
* ELA, 2-20 Kamiosaki, Shinagawa-ku, Tokyo; tel. 3491-4460.

* ELC; Tokyo, Toyoshima-ku, Sugamo 3-33; tel. 3910-6680.

* ELEC; 101, Tokyo, Chiyoda-ku, Kanda, 3-8 Jimbocho; tel. 3265-8911. Large school with all foreign teachers (100). All types of English taught.

* ELI; Tokyo, Toyoshima-ku, Higashi Ikebukuro, Osumi Bldg.; tel. 3980-0401.

* English Den, 5-14-7 Hirai Nakagawa, Edogawa-ku tel. 3617-7278.

* English House, 2-23 Nishi Ikebukuro, Tokyo; tel. 3988-1743.

* English House, 5-11 Hon, Nakano-ku, Tokyo; tel. 3383-6454.

* English House; Tokyo, Chiyoda-ku, Kanda, Kamiho, Noguchi Daini Bldg.; tel. 3291-5848.

* English Language Center, Ogawa Bldg., Jinbocho, Kanda, Tokyo; tel. 3295-2356.

* English Private School, 2-24 Ogibashi, Koto-ku, Tokyo; tel. 3645-1314.

* English Salon Jun; Tokyo, Minato-ku, Shin Hashinonaka Bldg.; tel. 3508-0473.

* English Service; 170, Tokyo, Higashi Ikebukuro 3-1-4, Maison Sunshine 1246; tel. 3988-3611. All foreign teachers (10).

* English Telephone Club, 136 Minami Oizumi, Nerima-ku, Tokyo; tel. 3924-3853.

* English Train; Tokyo, Minato-ku, Nishi Azabu 2-7; tel. 3486-9395.

* English Village, 3-10-10 Kamiosaki, Shinagawa-ku, Tokyo 141 tel. 3446-3837.

* ENL; Tokyo, Taito-ku, Moto Asakusa Kaibara Bldg.; tel. 3842-6357.

* Erokens Language School; Tokyo, Minato-ku, Ropponi 7-18; tel. 3405-7565.

* ESC; Tokyo, Setagaya-ku, Kamikitazawa 4-12; tel. 3329-3993.

* Espero Language School; Tokyo, Shibuya-ku, Yoyogi 1-57; tel. 3370-0399.

* Eternity; Tokyo, Shinjuku Rafu Kaikan; tel. 3350-6764.

* Eto Shingaku; Tokyo, Eto, Toyo 5-1; tel. 3645-4033.

* Euro Center Japan, Fukai Bldg., Surugadai, Kanda, Tokyo; tel. 3295-5441.
* Evergreen Eigo Gakuin; 150, Tokyo, Meguro-ku, 1-21-2 Yutenji; tel. 3713-4958. 7 foreign teachers.
* Excellence; 102, Tokyo, Chiyoda-ku, 4 Bancho 6, Palais Blanc 303. Personally recommended by a former teacher as being especially honest.
* Executive Gogaku Center; 107, Tokyo, Akasaka 1-9-20, Koa Dai 16 Bldg.; tel. 3585-6401. Large chain. 20 foreign teachers. Comparatively poor pay.
* Executive School; Tokyo, Chiyoda-ku, Kasumigaseki 3-2; tel. 3581-5631.
* FF Eigo Kyoshitsu, 3-1 Yoyogi, Tokyo; tel. 3375-5261.
* FIA, Fukumaru Bldg., 4-26-12 Minami Koenji, Suginami-ku, Tokyo 166 tel. 3314-6241.
* FIS; 155, Tokyo, Setagaya-ku, Kitazawa 2-10-15; tel. 3 468-8598. 13 foreign teachers.
* FJ Associates; Tokyo, Chuo-ku, Hachobori Fuji Bldg.; tel. 3553-5935.
* FL Center; 150, Tokyo, Shibuya-ku, Shibuya 2-19-20, Iwasaki Bldg. 3F; tel. 3400-9811. Well-known school with all foreign teachers (10). Experience required. .
* FL Center; Tokyo, Chiyoda-ku, Iidabashi 3-6; tel. 3262-5817.
* Fujimi English Conversation Gakuin, 2-4 Fujimi, Chiyoda-ku, Tokyo; tel. 3264-3957.
* Future Communication Center, Kami Ichi Bldg., Nishi Shinbashi, Minato-ku, Tokyo; tel. 3591-1436.
* Gaikokugo Noryoku Kaihatsu Center, Asahi Bldg., Uchikanda, Tokyo; tel. 3291-2288.
* Gakusei no Ie, 2-23-27 Hyakunin-cho, Shinjuku-ku, Tokyo; tel. 3362-2271.
* Gakusei no Ie; Tokyo, Toyoshima-ku, Mejiro 3-17; tel. 3950-8671.
* GEM; 150, Tokyo, Shibuya-ku, Shibuya 1-13-5, Daikyo Bldg. 4F; tel. 3406-8031. 15 foreign teachers.

* Genzai English School; Tokyo, Shibuya-ku, Yoyogi, Daini Nogi Bldg.; tel. 3370-2059.
* Ginza Beikaiwa Salon; 104, Tokyo, Chuo-ku 5-9-13 Nakamura Bldg.; tel. 3573-7427. All foreign teachers (19). ✓
* Global English Program; Tokyo, Minato-ku, Akasaka 2-16; tel. 3582-1679.
* Gogaku Jishu Kunrenjo, Yamaguchi Bldg., Higashi Ikebukuro, Tokyo; tel. 3982-2208.
* Gohoshi Gakuin; Tokyo, Minato-ku, Akasaka, Suzuki Bldg.; tel. 3582-5551.
* Goken Center; Tokyo, Minato-ku, Akasaka 9-1; tel. 3470-6546.
* Goodwill, 4-8 Takanawa, Minato-ku, Tokyo; tel. 3445-7845.
* Green English School; Tokyo, Shinagawa-ku, Nishi Gotanda 2-24; tel. 3492-2626.
* Greg School; Tokyo, Shibuya-ku, Dogenza-ka, Umehara Bldg.; tel. 3464-7481.
* Gregg/Tokyo Business School; 152, Tokyo, Meguro-ku, 1-14-16 Jugaoka; tel. 3724-0552. One of the largest schools with 102 foreign teachers. Features Business English.
* Gregg Language School; Chiyoda-ku, Kanda, Komakawadai, Segawa Bldg.; tel. 3295-4131.
* Hamamatsu School; Tokyo, Minato-ku, Hamamatsu, Sekai Boeki Bldg.; tel. 3435-5751.
* Hampton/Pan Pacific School of English, Daini Komatsu Bldg. 4F, 2-14-17 Shibuya, Tokyo 150; tel. 3406-1231. Instructors must have TEFL background. British preferred.
* Harajuku Gaigo Gakuin; 151, Tokyo, Shibuya-ku, Jingumae 5-11-8; tel. 3406-4604. 15 foreign teachers.
* Harajuku Language School; Tokyo, Shibuya-ku, Jingumae 5-11; tel. 3400-8695.
* Harold School; Suginami-ku, Koenji Kita 2-3; tel. 3338-5511.
* Harrison Language Service; Tokyo, Minato-ku, Roppongi 7-15; tel. 3423-1983.
* Hibiya Gakuin English School, 2-7 Higashi Gotanda, Shinagawa-ku, Tokyo; tel. 3442-9755.

* Hills Saino Kaihatsu Kenkyujo, 3-6 Higashi Yaguchi, Otaku, Tokyo; tel. 3734-2771.
* Honan English Academy; Tokyo, Suginami-ku, Honan 2-23; tel. 3313-1700.
* Horin Academia, FI Bldg. 6F, 1-26-5 Takadanobaba, Shinjuku-ku, Tokyo 160; tel. 3200-7771. Large school with 60 foreign teachers. Offers all types of English classes.
* IBS Harajuku, 6-31 Jingumae, Shibuya-ku, Tokyo; tel. 3486-7317.
* IBS; Tokyo, Minato-ku, Roppongi, Kyodo Bldg.; tel. 3404-1684.
* ICA; 171, Tokyo, Toyoshima-ku, Nishi Ikebukuro, 1-16-10; tel. 3984-2476. Related to San Antonio College.
* ICA; Tokyo, Toyoshima-ku, Minamai Otsuka, Yamate Bldg.; tel. 3947-6711.
* ICA; Tokyo, Toyoshima-ku, Nishi Ikebuku-ro, Mikasa Bldg.; tel. 3981-7988.
* ICCS, 1-15 Tabata, Kita-ku, Tokyo; tel. 3823-4394.
* ICE; Tokyo, Minato-ku, Akasaka 3-14; tel. 3584-2800.
* ICE; Tokyo, Minato-ku, Takanawa 4-7; tel. 3440-1800.
* ICF, 1-38 Akazutsumi, Setagaya-ku, Tokyo; tel. 3322-4726.
* IEI; Tokyo, Shinjuku-ku, Shimoochiai, Mejiro, Daiwada Bldg.; tel. 3952-8081.
* IF Gaigo Gakuin; 101, Tokyo, Chiyoda-ku, Kanda, Konya-cho 21-8; tel. 3252-7747. 5 foreign teachers.
* IHS; 171, Tokyo, Toyoshima-ku, Mejiro 2-34-3; tel. 3989-9851. International Hospitality Society. 30 foreign teachers.
* Ikeda Jinichi; Tokyo, Koto-ku, Toyo 3-16; tel. 3644-0680.
* IL Eigo Kyoshitsu, 1-49 Nishi Nippori, Arakawa-ku, Tokyo; tel. 3807-6414.
* ILC; 101, Tokyo, Chiyoda-ku, Jinden, Jimbocho 2-1, Iwanami Jimbocho Bldg. 9F; tel. 3954-5173. All foreign teachers (70), mostly British.

* ILS; Tokyo, Bunkyo-ku, Yayoi 2-7; tel. 3816-2503.

* InterEnglish School; Tokyo, Adachi-ku, Umeda 7-5; tel. 3852-1722.

* Interlang School and Service; 107, Tokyo, Kita-Aoyama 2-14-6, Bell Commons 7F; tel. 3497-5451. 15 foreign teachers using Interlang method.

* Interlingua Club; 154, Tokyo, Meguro-ku, Yutenji 2-15-17; tel. 3791-5561. 3 foreign teachers.

* Interlink; Tokyo, Minato-ku, Akasaka, Rokan Bldg.; tel. 3588-0022.

* Int'l Business Lang. Svc., Yanagiya Bldg., 1-16-6 Shinbashi, Minato-ku, Tokyo; tel. 3591-2770.

* Int'l Education Service, Shin Taiso Bldg., 2-10-7 Dogenzaka, Shibuya, Tokyo 150 tel. 3463-5396.

* Int'l Institute of Japan; 150, Tokyo, Jingumae 4-2-11, Belair Garden Bldg. 2F; tel. 3405-0754. 15 foreign teachers.

* InterTokyo; 107 Tokyo, Minato-ku, Akasaka 8-5-32, Yamakatsu Bldg. 7F; tel. 3479-4861. 2 foreign teachers.

* InterWorld; Tokyo, Minato-ku, Mita, Mitoyo Bldg.; tel. 3453-0343.

* InterWorld; Tokyo, Nishi Shinjuku, Hirata Bldg.; tel. 3371-5091.

* IPS; Tokyo, Shibuya-ku, Jingumae 6-31; tel. 3 400-7793.

* Ishikawa Gakuin; 124, Tokyo, Katsushika-ku, 3-29-12 Tateishi; tel. 3697-2222. Emphasizes practical English. 7 foreign teachers.

* ISS; 102, Tokyo, Chiyoda-ku, Kojimachi, 1-6 Sogo Daisan Bldg. Bekkan 5F; tel. 3265-7103. Famous business/translation school. 19 foreign teachers.

* IUE Eigo Gakuin, Kobayashi Bldg., 2-8-1 Minami Ikebukuro, Toshima-ku, Tokyo 171 tel. 3983-5466.

* Iwata Shokai; Tokyo, Nishi Shinjuku 3-5; tel. 3343-0247

* Japan Foreign Language Service, Ishikatsu Bldg., Minami Aoyama, Minato-ku, Tokyo; tel. 3479-2191.

* JEL Eigo Gakuin, 7-3 Todoroki, Setagaya-ku, Tokyo; tel. 3702-3828.
* Jido English School; Tokyo, Chuo-ku, Nihonbashi, Muro Ebiya Bldg.; tel. 3243-1960.
* Jishu School; Tokyo, Toyoshima-ku, Higashi Ikebukuro 1-17; tel. 3983-3483.
* Jiyu Foreign Language Center, Azusa Bldg., Todoroki, Setagaya-ku, Tokyo; tel. 3702-6771.
* Jiyu Language Center; Tokyo, Meguro-ku, Jiyugaoka 1-13; tel. 3723-3130.
* JPS Academy, Jingumae 6-31, Shibuya-ku, Tokyo; tel. 3406-5555. Highly accelerated classes.
* JPS Academy; 150, Tokyo, Shibuya-ku, Shibuya Home 1308, Udagawa-cho 2-1; tel. 3464-5555. 20 foreign teachers.
* Jugaoka Language School; 152, Tokyo, Meguro-ku, Jugaoka Depato, Jugaoka 1-28-8, tel. 3718-3926. 10 foreign teachers.
* Jumi Eigo Kai, 4-41 Sakuradai, Nerima-ku, Tokyo; tel. 3991-4548.
* Kaigai Bunka Center, Koei Bldg., 1-7-4 Uchikanda, Chiyoda-ku, Tokyo 101 tel. 3295-4110.
* Kaminoge Road Gakuin, Tamaya Bldg., Kaminoge, 2-5-21 Setagaya-ku, Tokyo 165 tel. 3704-4367.
* Kanda Gijitsu Academia, Morikyo Bldg. 1-2-9 Yoyogi, Shibuya-ku, Tokyo 151; tel. 3379-1795. Uses the direct method of instruction.
* Kanda Institute of Foreign Languages; 101, Tokyo, 2-13-13 Uchikanda; tel. 3254-2731. Largest school in Tokyo. 5,500 students, 94 foreign instructors.
* Kanrakuzaka Hearing Room; Tokyo, Shinjuku-ku, Kanrakuzaka 6-73; tel. 3267-2246.
* Kanrisha Yosei Gakko; 150, Tokyo, Nishi-Shimbashi 3-19-13, Tokyo Kensho Bldg.; tel. 3433-8351. 5 foreign teachers.
* Keio Center; Tokyo, Meguro, Jiyugaoka, Kameda Bldg.; tel. 3723-9475.
* Keishin Language School; 182, Tokyo, Chofu-shi, Senkawa-cho 1-2; tel. 3300-6885. Small classes. 9 foreign teachers.

* Kelly's English Lab; Tokyo, Shibuya-ku, Ebisu, Nishi Ogawa Bldg.; tel. 3496-2353.
* Kent Academy, Tokyo, Shibuya-ku, Hiroo 5-4; tel. 3442-2938. Their motto: "Face to Face."
* Kent English School; Tokyo, Shibuya-ku, Ebisu, Minami 1-6; tel. 3711-3903.
* Kent House; Tokyo, Tamagawa Denenchofu 1-14; tel. 3721-5311.
* Kent School; 150, Tokyo, Shibuya-ku, Ebisu Minami 1-6-3; tel. 3713-7046. 16 foreign teachers.
* Keto English School; Tokyo, Setagaya-ku, Sakuragaoka 2-10; tel. 3426-2890.
* Kilby Gakuin; 160, Tokyo, Shinjuku-ku, Nishi-Shinjuku 1-21-1, Myoho Bldg. 5F; tel. 3342-6001. Features singing and dance classes. 8 foreign teachers.
* KLG; Tokyo, Meguro 1-12; tel. 3493-8863.
* Kodo Language School; Tokyo, Chiyoda-ku, Rokubancho 13-2; tel. 3261-1971.
* Koei Gakuin Kamedo Kyoshitsu, Tamagawaya Bldg., Kamedo, Koto-ku, Tokyo; tel. 3684-4371.
* Koike Trading Management; Tokyo, Shinjuku-ku, Minami Moto 4-40; tel. 3355-1621.
* Kokusai Bunkya Center; Tokyo, Nerima-ku, Toyodamakita 5-16; tel. 3993-4321.
* Kokusai Bunkya Kyokai; Tokyo, Chiyoda-ku, Kudankita 1-9; ; tel. 3265-1407.
* Kokusai Business College; 150, Tokyo, 3-17-2 Shibuya-ku, Kaneda Bldg.; tel. 3409-1981. Secretarial school with 10 foreign teachers.
* Kokusai Eigo Gakkoo, 1-29-5 Yoyogi, Shibuya-ku, Tokyo 151 tel. 3370-0571.
* Kokusai Eiken Center; 158, Tokyo, Setagaya-ku, Seda 1-19-2, Akira Mansion; tel. 3709-7688. All foreign teachers (10).
* Kokusai English School; Tokyo, Edogawa-ku, Higashi Komatsugawa 1-12; tel. 3655-6680.
* Kokusai Gakuin, Riyobi Bldg. 3F, 2-10-11 Kajimachi, Kanda, Chiyoda-ku, Tokyo; tel. 3252-0956.
* Kokusai Gogaku Center; Tokyo, Taito-ku, Ueno Kawamura Bldg.; tel. 3842-5737.

* Kokusai Kenshukai; Tokyo, Chuo-ku, Ginza, Daini Namiya Bldg.; tel. 3572-3166.

* Kokusai Kyoiku Kabu, Totoru Bldg., Higashi Azabu, Tokyo; tel. 3586-5331.

* Kokusai Renmei, Chisanamu Peidai, 24-8 Sakuragaoka-cho, Shibuya-ku, Tokyo 150 tel. 3496-2041. Primarily translation and interpreting classes.

* Kokusai Ryugaku Center; Tokyo, Shibuya, Oyama Bldg.; tel. 3986-0221.

* Kokusai Seinen Inkai; Tokyo, Chiyoda-ku, Nagata-cho, Sanno Grand Bldg.; tel. 3592-0940.

* Kokusai Shinzen; Tokyo, Shibuya-ku, Nishiwara 3-37; tel. 3466-3028.

* Kokusai Shuriman; Tokyo, Shinjuku, Sanei, Bonaflower Bldg.; tel. 3355-1168.

* Komagata English School; Tokyo, Taito-ku, Komagata 2-3; tel. 3844-8310.

* Korakuen English Center, Koraku 1-3, Bunkyo-ku, Tokyo 112; tel. 3811-2111. British English preferred but will consider North Americans.

* Kubo Takao; Tokyo, Toyoshima-ku, Kamiikebukuro 3-44; tel. 3916-1403.

* Kyodo Weston School, Yuwa Bldg., 2-3-12 Kitazawa, Setagaya-ku, Tokyo 155 tel. 3412-3065.

* Language Training Service; Tokyo, Minato-ku, Shinbashi, Sogo Bldg.; tel. 3574-7032.

* Lauren Language School; Tokyo, Setagaya-ku, Sangenjaya 1-19; tel. 3421-1852.

* LC Language Club, 3-16-19 Roppongi, Minato-ku, Tokyo; tel. 3584-2813.

* LIC; Tokyo, Shibuya-ku, Dogenzaka 2-15; tel. 3 476-1051.

* Lingua Gakuin, Yuki Bldg. 3-303, 2-19-1 Koenji Minami, Suginami-ku, Tokyo 166; tel. 3312-2377. Small school with 2 foreign teachers.

* Linguarama; Akasaka Heights #401, 9-5-26 Akasaka, Minato-ku, Tokyo 107; tel. 3403-5724. All foreign teachers (9) offer assortment of classes.

* Lombard School, Yajima Bldg., Yotsuya, Shinjuku-ku, Tokyo; tel. 3358-6692.

* LS Language Study, 2-24 Kami Osaki, Shinagawa-ku, Tokyo; tel. 3493-0837.
* Lutheran School; 1-2-32 Fujimi, Chiyoda-ku, Tokyo 102; tel. 3263-9835. American Lutheran Church. 10 foreign teachers.
* Mary Pearl English School; Tokyo, Toyoshima-ku, Higashi Ikebukuro, Kaneko Bldg.; tel. 3982-1938.
* Matsudo Eikaiwa, Kurokawa Bldg. 5F, 3-4 Sakuragaoka-cho, Shibuya-ku, Tokyo 150; tel. 3496-0555. Has own method, stressing "mental attitude."
* Matsumoto Eigo Semmon Gakkoo, Shibuya 1-4-8, Shibuya-ku, Tokyo 150; tel. 3400-8321. 5 foreign teachers use "spartan" approach to learning.
* Matsumoto English School; Tokyo, Shibuya 1-4; tel. 3499-3381.
* Matsumoto English School; Tokyo, Suginami-ku, Onya 1-17; tel. 3317-5316.
* McNall Foreign Language Gakuin, Shimada Bldg., Minami Koiwa, Edogawa-ku, Tokyo; tel. 3672-0201.
* Meguro Conversation Gakuin, 4-3 Kami Osaki, Shinagawa-ku, Tokyo; tel. 3493-7203.
* Meguro English Classroom, 5-22 Shirogane-dai, Minato-ku, Tokyo; tel. 3440-1921.
* Meguro School, Itaki Bldg. 3F, 2-15-15 Kamiosaki, Shinagawa-ku, Tokyo 141; tel. 3446-2181. Small classes for 5 foreign teachers.
* Meizen Gakuin, English School, 4-20 Kita Omori, Tokyo; tel. 3761-1124.
* Mesenkai Culture Center; Tokyo, Shinjuku-ku, Minami Moto 6-2; tel. 3351-0297.
* Metro Gakuin, 1-18 Ichiyada, Tokyo; tel. 3260-6122.
* Mia American School; 162, Tokyo, Shinjuku-ku, Sumiyoshi-cho 108, OSK Bldg. 701; tel. 3358-1475. 10 foreign teachers.
* Mia Creative Academy, Edogawa-ku, Tokyo; tel. 3687-4896.
* Milestone Organization; Tokyo, Shibuya-ku, Jingumae 4-31; tel. 3423-2551.

* Mimizuku English School; Tokyo, Shibuya-ku, Uehara 3-4; ; tel. 3468-6818.
* Miniko; Nakao Bldg. 1-29-8 Komagome, Toshima-ku, Tokyo 170. tel. 3945-1691.
* Mita English Gakuin, 5-17 Komazawa, Setagaya-ku, Tokyo; tel. 3704-4947.
* Model Language Studio, Yasuto Bldg. 1-43-7 Yoyogi, Shibuya-ku, Tokyo 151; tel. 3370-7843. Stresses "live" English. 3 foreign teachers.
* Myosenkai Culture Center; 160, Tokyo, Shinjuku-ku, Minami Motomachi 6-2; tel. 3351-0297. All foreign teachers (15).
* Naganuma School, 16-26 Nanpeidai, Shibuya-ku, Tokyo 150 tel. 3463-7261.
* Nakajima Eigo Semmon Kyoshitsu, Nakaya Bldg., Shin Koiwa, Katsushikaku, Tokyo; tel. 3651-6791.
* NASA; 160, Tokyo, Shinjuku-ku, Takadano-baba 2-14-5; tel. 3200-9731. 5 foreign teachers.
* NCB, Shinjuku Center Bldg., 1-25-1 Nishi-Shinjuku, Shinjuku-ku, Tokyo 160 tel. 3342-5335.
* Nichibei Kaiwa Gakuin, Yotsuya 1-21, Shinjuku-ku, Tokyo 160; tel. 3359-9621. Prestigious school. 65 instructors, American English.
* Nicholai Gakkuin, 4-1 Surugadai, Kanda, Chiyoda-ku, Tokyo 101; tel. 3291-9057. Founded in 1873.
* Nihon Business School, 6-7-13 Minami Aoyama, Minato-ku, Tokyo 107; tel. 3400-2141. Teaches secretarial/trading skills, 110 foreign teachers.
* Nihon Gakuin Tsugakubu, Sohyo Kaikan 3F, 3-2-11 Surugadai, Kanda, Tokyo-to; tel. 3251-4735. Translation school with small foreign teaching staff (2).
* Nihon Gakuin; 162, Tokyo, Shinjuku-ku, Agebacho 20, Daini Tobundo Bldg.; tel. 3267-1331. 20 foreign teachers.
* Nihon Kagaku Honyaku Kyokai, Haruki Bldg., Kita Aoyama, Minato-ku, Tokyo; tel. 3403-8811.

* Nihon Kenkyujo; 160, Tokyo, Shibuya-ku, Yoyogi 2-23-1, New State Manor 1172; tel. 3370-3454. 18 foreign teachers.

* Nihon Kyoiku System; Tokyo, Shinjuku-ku, Nishi Shinjuku Toyo Bldg.; tel. 3348-7951.

* Nihon Kyokai; Tokyo, Toyoshima-ku, Higashi Ikebukuro, Osumi Bldg.; tel. 3986-3689.

* Nihon Resco; Tokyo, Shibuya-ku, Yoyogi 1-28; tel. 3 374-2721.

* Nihon Tsuyaku Yoseijo; 152, Tokyo, Shinagawa-ku, Kamiosaki 3-1-5, Eki Bldg. 8F; tel. 3440-4651. 8 foreign teachers for primarily translation students.

* Nino Carter Academy; Tokyo, Minato-ku, Akasaka 3-11; tel. 3587-1941.

* Nippori Language Center; Tokyo, Arakawa-ku, Nishi Nippori 4-21-3; tel. 3824-2401.

* Nishiyama Kikuko Eigo Kyoshitsu, 5-20 Higashi Koiwa, Edogawa-ku, Tokyo; tel. 3671-5282.

* Nisseito English Center; Tokyo, Adachi-ku, Aoi 4-1; tel. 3848-3217.

* Nisseito; Tokyo, Toyoshima-ku, Mejiro 3-17; tel. 3950-1111.

* Novice Foreign Language Gakuin, Sky Bldg., Kita Aoyama, Minato-ku, Tokyo; tel. 3404-8888.

* NSS Gaigo Gakuin, 6-13 Akasaka, Tokyo; tel. 3586-2997.

* Obunsha LL Kyoshitsu, 3-32 Narimasu, Itabashi-ku, Tokyo; tel. 3939-5703.

* Ogami English School; Tokyo; tel. 3623-0863.

* Omura Gaigo Gakuin, Hongo Medical Bldg., Bunkyo-ku, Tokyo; tel. 3816-1761.

* Ono English School, 9-18 Kita Karasuyama, Setagaya-ku, Tokyo; tel. 3307-0509.

* Orikon English School; Tokyo, Chuo-ku, Ginza, Suyoroya Bldg.; tel. 3571-6049.

* OSCC; 101, Tokyo, Chiyoda-ku, Kanda, 2-1 Surugadai; tel. 3291-1285. Emphasizes Bible teaching. All foreign teachers (10).

* Otani Chifumi; Tokyo, Shinagawa-ku, Osaki 4-1; tel. 3492-4053.

* OTC; Tokyo, Chuo-ku, Yaesu Kotobuki Bldg.; tel. 3275-0341.

* Oyama English School; Tokyo, Minato-ku, Moto Azabu 3-1; ; tel. 3403-8950.

* PACC, Dai San Shikakura Bldg., 1-7 Yotsuya, Shinjuku-ku, Tokyo 160 tel. 3353-1771.

* Pacific English Club, 1-29 Hamadayama, Suginami-ku, Tokyo; tel. 3303-6764.

* Pacific Language School, 2-29 Higashi Takaido, Suginami-ku, Tokyo; tel. 3334-2849.

* Pacific Language School, Hikaru Bldg., Komaba, Meguro-ku, Tokyo; tel. 3465-9909.

* Pan Academic School; Tokyo, Shibuya-ku, Jingumae 1-17; tel. 3478-5140.

* Pan World; Tokyo, Setagaya-ku, Seijo 2-40; tel. 3416-2391.

* Panalingua, 1-43 Yoyogi, Tokyo; tel. 3370-7105.

* PE American Club, Ogikubo Bldg. 9F, 5-27-8 Ogikubo, Suginami-ku, Tokyo 167; tel. 3393-4391.

* Pearl English School; Tokyo; Nakano-ku, Matsugaoka 1-3; tel. 3389-7347.

* Peck English Salon; Tokyo, Shinjuku, Shinjuku HK Bldg.; tel. 3356-1312.

* Pegasus Language Service, Sankei Bldg. Shinkan, Ote, Tokyo; tel. 3244-4247.

* Pentagon English School; Tokyo, Shibuya, Miyano Bldg.; tel. 3409-7200.

* PGK English Lounge; Tokyo, Nakano 5-52; tel. 3385-7011.

* Pinocchio English Conversation Classroom, 6-8 Ikegami, Tokyo; tel. 3752-0361.

* Prade House; Tokyo, Minato-ku, Akasaka, New Akasaka Bldg.; tel. 3584-2561.

* Prade House; Tokyo, Minato-ku, Akasaka 3-2; tel. 3584-2569.

* Prade House; Tokyo, Toyoshima-ku, Higashi Ikebukuro 3-2; ; tel. 3989-8135.

* Progre, Sanwa Bldg., Fujimi, Chiyoda-ku, Tokyo; tel. 3262-0087.

* Queen's English Conversation School, Okayama Bldg., 3-33-7 Kita Senaoku, Tokyo; tel. 3728-2351.

* Renaissance Eigo Gakuin; 150, Tokyo, Shibuya 1-24-7, Miyashita Park Bldg.; tel. 3407-8466. 5 foreign teachers.

* Richard Conversation Seminar, 2-48-12 Denen Chofu, Ota-ku, Tokyo; tel. 3721-3206.

* Ripitomeku School; 160, Tokyo, Shinjuku-ku, Shinano-cho 34, Toshin Bldg. 2F; 6 foreign instructors emphasize listening and speaking.

* Robert Gaigo Gakuin; 151, Tokyo, Shibuya-ku, Sendagaya 3-61-7; tel. 3401-0067. 25 foreign teachers.

* Robert's English Center; Tokyo, Setagaya-ku, Sangenjaya 1-39; tel. 3424-9765.

* Royal English Seminar, 2-16 Todoroki, Setagaya-ku, Tokyo; tel. 3702-1824.

* Runashian Academy, 3-9 Umejima, Adachi-ku, Tokyo; tel. 3887-4510.

* Saimaru Academy; 106, Tokyo, Minato-ku, 1-5-17 Roppongi; tel. 3582-9841. 20 foreign teachers. Emphasizes simultaneous translation.

* Salon Academy; 151, Tokyo, Shibuya-ku, Yoyogi 2-6-7, Seichi Bldg. 4F; tel. 3379-5661. All foreign teachers (15).

* San Luis Language Center, 2-15 Dogenzaka, Shibuya-ku, Tokyo; tel. 3464-9165.

* Sankei International College, 1-7-2 Shimbunsha Honkan, Otemachi, Tokyo 100 tel. 3246-0634. Classes are transferable to certain US universities.

* Sankei International College; 152, Tokyo, Meguro-ku, Hibumidani 5-9-8; tel. 3794-1761. 10 foreign teachers.

* SDA; 167, Tokyo, Suginami-ku, Tensho 3-17-3; tel. 3392-0419. All foreign teachers (11).

* Seijo School; Tokyo, Setagaya-ku, Seijo 2-8; tel. 3416-4136.

* Shane English School; Tokyo, Edogawa-ku, Nishi Kuzunishi, Amafuji Bldg.; tel. 3689-4143.

* Shane English School; Tokyo, Shibuya-ku, Ebisu Nishi 1-8; tel. 3463-1064.
* Shenandoah Eigo Juku, 1-39 Minami Tokiwadai, Itabashi-ku, Tokyo; tel. 3956-4542.
* Shibuya Gaigo Gakuin; 150, Tokyo, Shibuya-ku, Sakuragaoka-cho 15-15; tel. 3461-8854. 8 foreign teachers.
* Shimada Eikaiwa Kenkyujo; 171, Tokyo, Toyoshima-ku, Minami-Nagasaki 1-14-8; tel. 3952-0061. Specializes in voice training. 1 foreign teacher.
* Shinagawa Foreign Language School, 3-25 Takanawa, Minato-ku, Tokyo; tel. 3447-7550.
* Shinjuku Kyoiku Kaikan, 7-22 Nishi Shinjuku, Tokyo; tel. 3363-1641.
* Shiragiku School; Tokyo, Itabashi-ku, Toshin 2-3; tel. 3958-7171.
* Shuwa English School, 1-17 Sugamo, Toshima-ku, Tokyo; tel. 3947-9945.
* Simulax; Tokyo, Shibuya-ku, Sendagaya, Kagaku Kogyosha Bldg.; tel. 3423-0281.
* SLS; Tokyo, Minato-ku, Roppongi, Maki Bldg.; tel. 3582-9948.
* SMI; Tokyo, Shinjuku 1-9; tel. 3356-1977.
* Smith-Okayama English Conversation School, 2-4 Okayama, Meguro-ku, Tokyo; tel. 3717-5907.
* Sokusei Iris Kyoshitsu, Residence Bldg., Kamiosaki Shuwa, Shinagawa-ku, Tokyo. tel.445-1994. Many types of English classes taught.
* Sony Eigo Kyoshitsu; 160, Tokyo, Kurihara Bldg. 7F, 1-6-12 Nishi Shimbashi; tel. 3232-0290. Affiliated with Sony Corp. 40 unionized foreign teachers.
* Sony LL Shibuya, Kami Minami Bldg., 4-3 Udagawa-cho, Shibuya-ku, Tokyo; tel. 3461-9257.
* Sophia English Gakuin, 2-42 Minami Otsuka, Toshima-ku, Tokyo; tel. 3947-9317.
* SSS, 3-22 Aobadai, Meguro-ku, Tokyo; tel. 3793-5730.
* SSS, Hongo, Bunkyo-ku, Tokyo; tel. 3815-5844.
* SSS Institute, 10-9 Kami Izumi, Shibuya-ku, Tokyo; tel. 3496-5730.

* SSS, Soma Bldg., Kamiuma, Setagaya-ku, Tokyo; tel. 3424-6032.
* SSS, Toto Bldg., Higashi Ikebukuro, Tokyo; tel. 3988-6032.
* Stanton School of English; 102, Tokyo, Chiyoda-ku, Rokuban-cho 7; tel. 3262-3300. All British teachers (30) with TEFL license.
* Study Corner, Yutaka Bldg., Shimo Takaido, Suginami-ku, Tokyo; tel. 3322-1787.
* Successful English School, Towa Bldg., 515 Higashi Oizumi, Nerima-ku, Tokyo 188 tel. 3923-7249.
* Sun Academy, 1-4 Minami Akabane, Tokyo; tel. 3903-3764.
* Sun Language School; Tokyo, Shibuya 3-25; tel. 3407-7423.
* Sun Life; 160, Tokyo, Shinjuku-ku, Takadanobaba 4-11-13, Art Daiichi Bldg. 2F; tel. 3367-4881. 20 foreign teachers.
* Sunbright Telephone Group; 105, Tokyo, Minato-ku, Shiba 3-22-7, CBC Bldg.; tel. 3451-1851. Lessons given by telephone, 34 teachers.
* Sundai ELS Eigo Gakuin; 101, Tokyo, Chiyoda-ku, Kanda, 1-5-8 Surugadai; tel. 3233-2311. Part of the world-wide ELS chain. 9 foreign teachers.
* Sunshine Business Gakko; 170, Tokyo, Toyoshima-ku, Higashi Ikebukuro 4-23-4; tel. 3987-5611. 14 foreign teachers. School emphasizes business courses.
* Sunshine Gaigo Gakko; 170, Tokyo, Higashi Ikebukuro 3-1-1, Sunshine Bldg. 9F; tel. 3987-1921. 5 foreign teachers. Relatively poor pay.
* Tatsunoko Culture Center, 3-16 Nishi Nippori, Tokyo; tel. 3824-4804.
* Terry's Children's Society, 3-30 Gohongi, Meguro-ku, Tokyo; tel. 3711-5004.
* TES; 103, Tokyo, Chuo-ku, Nihonbashi, Kodenba-cho 5-15; tel. 3663-8771. Business school with 12 foreign teachers.
* Tespa English Conversation School, 2-22 Kitazawa, Setagaya-ku, Tokyo; tel. 3414-4444.

* THE English School; Tokyo, Shibuya-ku, Jingumae 1-9; ; tel. 3470-2457.
* Think Right English School; Tokyo, Shibuya-ku, Maruyama 15; tel. 3461-4472.
* Thomas Gaigo Gakuin, 1-17 Jinbocho, Kanda, Chiyoda-ku, Tokyo; tel. 3291-9341.
* TIE English Conversation Club, 31 Sakuragaoka, Shibuya-ku, Tokyo; tel. 33496-6049.
* Time-Life Lang. Center, Time-Life Bldg. 1F, 2-3-6 Otemachi, Chiyoda-ku, Tokyo; tel. 3279-4370/270-6611.
* TIS, 1-3 Tsutsujigaoka, Chofu-shi, Tokyo; tel. 3307-4367.
* TOEFL Academy, New State Mena 2F, 2-23-1 Yoyogi, Shibuya-ku, Tokyo 151; tel. 3375-2307. 18 foreign teachers prepare students for the TOEFL exam.
* TOEFL Seminar; 160, Tokyo, Shinjuku-ku, Takadanobaba 4-13-10; tel. 3371-4391. 20 foreign teachers.
* Toho Gakuen Semmon Gakkoo, 2-4-1 Izumi, Suginami-ku, Tokyo 168; tel. 3323-8531. Affiliated with San Francisco Univ. 4 foreign teachers.
* Tokyo Academy; 141, Tokyo, Shinagawa-ku, Kamiosaki 2-15-14, Takagi Bldg. 5F; tel. 3440-7227. All foreign teachers (14).
* Tokyo Business College, Paris Saido Bldg. 1F, Hitotsubashi 1-1-1, Tokyo 100; tel. 3213-0962. Business school for import/-export. 8 foreign teachers.
* Tokyo English Conversation School, 3-20 Nishi Arai, Adachi-ku, Tokyo; tel. 3853-2501.
* Tokyo English Community Center; Tokyo, Shinjuku-ku, Takadanobaba 2-14-27; tel. 3207-4421.
* Tokyo English House; Tokyo, Suginami-ku, Shoan 3-17; tel. 3332-0940.
* Tokyo English House; Tokyo, Nakano-ku, Minamidai 3-46; tel. 3384-0918.
* Tokyo Foreign Language Gakuin, Taguchi Bldg., Tomioka, Koto-ku, Tokyo; tel. 3641-5789.

* Tokyo Foreign Language College; 7-3-8 Nishi Shinjuku, Shinjuku-ku, Tokyo 160; tel. 3367-1101. Has a large foreign teaching staff (46).

* Tokyo Jido Gakuin; Tokyo, Chiyoda-ku, Kanda, Sakuma Sankyo Bldg.; tel. 3866-8915.

* Tokyo Julius Gakuin, Kobayashi Dai Ni Bldg., Ningyo, Nihonbashi, Tokyo; tel. 3668-5636.

* Tokyo Kogakuin Gaigo Gakkoo; 161, Tokyo, Shinjuku-ku, Shimo-ochiai 1-1-8; tel. 3360-0341. 9 foreign teachers. Prefers British with experience.

* Tokyo Kokusai Gakuen Mejiro-ko, 3-20 Shimo Ochiai, Shinjuku-ku, Tokyo; tel. 3954-1797.

* Tokyo Language Center; Tokyo, Shibuya, Sanshin Bldg.; tel. 3486-7661.

* Tokyo Language Center; Tokyo; Chuo-ku, Ginza, Dai Nichi Bldg.; tel. 3543-6830.

* Tokyo School of Business; Yoyogi 1-56, Shibuya-ku, Tokyo 151; tel. 3370-2222. Emphasizes business ESL. 5 foreign teachers.

* Tokyo Suginami Eigo Gakko; 166, Tokyo, Suginami-ku, Koenji Minami 4-44-12; tel. 3314-2435. 4 foreign students.

* Tokyo Yamanote YMCA Eigo Gakoin, 2-18-12 Nishi Waseda, Shinjuku-ku, Tokyo 160. 9 foreign teachers use "living English" with role play and conversation.

* Tokyo YMCA Eigo Semmon Gakkoo, Mitoyo-cho 7, Kanda, Chiyoda-ku, Tokyo 101; tel. 3293-9471. Emphasizes culture and customs. 34 foreign teachers.

* Tokyo YWCA Semmon Gakkoo, 1-8 Surugadai, Kanda, Chiyoda-ku, Tokyo 101; tel. 3293-5421. 18 foreign teachers instruct mostly female students.

* Tommy Uematsu Language Center, 2-23 Yoyogi, Tokyo; tel. 3374-5055.

* Travel Journal Ryokoo Gakkoo, 4-6-6 Higashi Nakano, Nakano-ku, Tokyo 164; tel. 3367-8111. Travel school with 9 foreign teachers.

* Trendom, 2-5-4 Nishi Ebisu, Shibuya-ku, Tokyo; tel. 3464-0077.

* Trendom; Tokyo, Shibuya-ku, Ebisu, Minami Wakaba Bldg.; tel. 3792-3321.

* Tsuda School of Business; 1-18-24 Sendagaya, Shibuya-ku, Tokyo 151; tel. 3402-7331. Business-oriented curriculum. 14 foreign teachers.
* Tsutsujigaoka Gaigo Gakuin, Sasaki Bldg., Tsutsujigaoka, Higashi Fuchu, Tokyo; tel. 3308-4302.
* Tsuyaku Gaido Yoseijo; 171, Tokyo, Toshima-ku, Takada 3-36-1; tel. 3988-6141. Emphasizes translation training. 30 foreign teachers.
* Tsuyaku Guide; Tokyo, Shinjuku-ku, Takadanobaba SKH Bldg.; tel. 3200-4011.
* TT Conversation; Tokyo, Shinjuku-ku, Araki 11; tel. 3351-5908.
* Turner English Conversation School, Mikado Bldg., Otsuka, Bunkyo-ku, Tokyo; tel. 3944-2951.
* Uni College; 101, Tokyo, Chiyoda-ku, Kanda, Jinbocho 1-19, Narita Bldg.; tel. 3291-7630. 3 foreign teachers.
* Universal Japan; Tokyo, Chuo-ku, Ginza, Mifuku Bldg.; tel. 3561-6467.
* Universal Sangyo Gogaku Kenkyujo, Fujibo Kaikan, Fujimi, Chiyoda-ku, Tokyo; tel. 3234-5071.
* USA Information Center; Tokyo, Shibuya-ku, Jingumae 1-2; tel. 3408-2901.
* Valentine Road English School, Ishizawa Bldg., Jiyugaoka, Meguro-ku, Tokyo; tel. 3724-6543.
* Warwick English Conversation School, 1-3 Nishi Azabu, Tokyo; tel. 3479-4545.
* Washington English Academy, Kugayama Bldg., Kugayama, Suginami-ku, Tokyo; tel. 3332-1258.
* Watson English Kenshujo, Matsuhide Bldg., Koishikawa, Bunkyo-ku, Tokyo; tel. 3947-0745.
* WCL Eifutsu Gogakuin, 3-7-4 Mejiro, Toshima-ku, Tokyo; tel. 3953-5930.
* West Eikaiwa Gakuin, 7-5 Akatsuka, Itabashi-ku, Tokyo; tel. 3938-2906.
* West Virginia University; 102, Tokyo, Chiyoda-ku, Gobancho 4-2, Topre Bldg.; tel. 3234-0357. All foreign teachers (10).
* Will English School; Tokyo, Minato-ku, Shiba 2-5; tel. 3454-7737.

\* Williams Academy; 150, Tokyo, Shibuya-ku, Jingumae 6-5-3, Ga-Z Bldg. 4F; tel. 3486-1248. 12 foreign teachers.

\* WINS; 160, Tokyo, Shinjuku-ku, Nishi-Shinjuku 2-1-1, Mitsui Bldg. 49F; tel. 3344-4882. 14 foreign teachers.

\* World English School; Tokyo, Adachi-ku, Nishi Arai, Hon 1-17; tel. 3854-5475.

\* World Languages Gakuin, Tokiwa Sogo Bldg., Kamiminami, Shibuya-ku, Tokyo; tel. 3464-1161.

\* Yaesu School; Tokyo, Chuo-ku, Yaesu, Sumitomo Seimei Yaesu Bdlg.; tel. 3274-3051.

\* Yamaoka International, 5426 Oizumi Gakuen, Nerima-ku, Tokyo; tel. 3923-8888.

\* Yamaoka International Academy, 3-12 Kita Aoyama, Minato-ku, Tokyo; tel. 3406-3144.

\* Yamate American English Conversation Gakuin, 2-29 Ohara, Setagaya-ku, Tokyo; tel. 3328-3558.

\* Yamate Eikaiwa School, 2-19-18 Shibuya, Shibuya-ku, Tokyo 150; tel. 3400-5025. Small classes. All foreign teachers (10).

\* York English School; Tokyo, Toyoshima-ku, Higashi Ikebukuro 3-15; tel. 3984-0360.

\* York Kenkyujo; Tokyo, Meguro-ku, Kakinokizaka 2-15; tel. 3718-6330.

\* Yoshida English Classroom, 3-26 Nishi Ochiai, Shinjuku-ku, Tokyo; tel. 3951-0528.

\* Yoshida English Center; Tokyo, Shinjuku-ku, Nishi Ochibori 2-15; tel. 3951-0355.

\* Yotsuya Gaigo Gakuin, PL Yotsuya Bldg., Motoshio-cho 9, Shinjuku-ku, Tokyo 160; tel. 3341-1434. Stresses "practical" English. 20 foreign instructors.

\* Yoyogi Mariko, 2-2 Asagaya Kita, Suginami-ku, Tokyo; tel. 3338-3044.

\* Zora Language Center, 1-21 Jingumae, Shibuya-ku, Tokyo; tel. 3402-8649.

## KANTO AREA

* AES; 243, Kanagawa-ken, Atsugi-shi,
Nakamachi 3-18-14; tel. 0462-24-3511. All foreign
teachers (20).
* Asahi Culture Center; 220, Kanagawa-ken,
Yokohama-shi, Nishi-ku, Takashima 2-16-1, Yokohama
Lumine Bldg.; tel. 045-453-1122. 40 foreign teachers.
* Berlitz School, Sky Bldg. 6F, 5-203
Motomachi, Naka-ku, Yokohama 231; tel. 045-651-2891.
See description of Berlitz above.
* Chiba YMCA Eigo Gakuin, Chiba, Masago
5-20-5; tel. 0472-79-8411. 3 foreign teachers.
* Cosmos Gogaku Center; 221, Kanagawa-ken,
Yokohama-shi, Kanagawa-ku, Nishi-Kanagawa 1-3-6,
Coop Fuji 605; tel. 045-321-2621. 2
foreign teachers.
* Cosmopolitan; 220, Yokohama, Nishi-ku
2-11-2, Sky Manor 405; tel. 045-453-2620. Small
school with one foreign teacher.
* Designer Gakuin; 220, Yokohama,
Kanagawa-ku, Daimachi 22-14; 3 foreign teachers.
Emphasizes hotel and travel English.
* East-West Gaikokugo Semmon Gakko; 281,
Chiba, Inagedai-cho 18-10; tel. 0472-43-7611. 4
foreign teachers.
* English House Gakuin, 4-22-1 Chiyogaoka,
Kawasaki-shi 215; tel. 044-955-0809. 5 foreign
teachers.
* Fujisawa Gaigo Center, Hirota Bldg. 2F & 3F,
Fujisawa 976, Fujisawa-shi, Kanagawa-ken; tel.
0466-26-0203. 19 foreign teachers emphasize
speaking.
* Gaigo Business Semmon Gakko; 210,
Kanagawa-ken, Kawasaki-shi, Eki Mae Honcho 22-9;
tel. 044-244-1959. 47 foreign teachers and broad
curriculum.
* Gogaku Kenshu Center; 221, Kanagawa-ken,
Yokohama-shi, Kanagawa-ku, Tsuruya-cho 3-32,
Academia Bldg.; tel. 045-311-5361. 35 foreign
teachers.

* Hioshi Eigo Gakuin, 1778 Hiyoshi Hommachi, Kohoku-ku, Yokohama 220; tel. 044-61-7040. 4 foreign students.

* JCC Academy; 223, Yokohama, Minato Kita-ku, Hiyoshi Motomachi 1867-1, Hiyoshi Center Bldg. 3F; tel. 044-63-6469. 2 foreign teachers.

* Kansai Gaigo Gakuin; 640, Wakayama, Nishi Takamatsu 1-5-1; tel. 0734-36-5694. 2 foreign teachers.

* LIOJ; 250, Kanagawa-ken, Odawara-shi, Shiroyama 4-14-1, Asia Center Nai; tel. 0465-23-1667. All foreign teachers (20). Training/experience required.

* Mobara Eigo Gakuin; 297; Chiba-ken, Mobara-shi, Takashi 619-11; tel. 0475-22- 4785. Very small school with 1 foreign teacher.

* QE Eikaiwa Gakuin; 272, Chiba-ken, Ichikawa-shi, Minami Yawata 4-7-14, Yugetsu Bldg. 3F; tel. 0473-77-1143. 6 foreign teachers.

* Seimei Bldg. 4F; tel. 045-311-5803. 9 foreign teachers.

* Shonan English College, 1-2-2 Kobukuro-dai, Kamakura-shi, Kanagawa-ken 247; tel. 0467-46-7370. 6 foreign teachers.

* Sony Eigo Kyoshitsu; 220, Yokohama, Kanagawa-ku, Tsuruya-cho 2-25-2, Mitsui Seimei Bldg. 4F; tel. 045-311-5803. 9 foreign teachers.

* Yamate Eigakuin, 1-36 Hinode-cho, Naka-ku, Yokohama-shi, Kanagawa-ken; tel. 045-231-1841. 3 foreign teachers.

* Yokohama Academy, Academy Bldg., Tsuruyakucho 3-32, Kanagawa-ku, Yokohama 221; tel. 045-311-5361. Oldest secretarial school in Japan. 35 foreign teachers.

* Yokohama Gaigo Business College, Yamanote-cho 45, Naka-ku, Yokohama 231; tel. 045-641-3919. Large business school. 11 foreign teachers.

* Yokohama YMCA Gakuin, 1-7 Joban-cho, Naka-ku, Yokohama 231; tel. 045-662-3721. 24 foreign teachers. See YMCA description above.

# CENTRAL HONSHU

* Colorado Eigo Gakuin; 676, Hyogo-ken, Takasago-shi, Yoneda-cho, Yonedashin 20-3; tel. 0794-31-6507. 2 foreign teachers.

* English Center; 430, Shizuoka-ken, Hamamatsu-shi, Toshimachi 11, Kawai Bldg.; tel. 0534-56-0109. 8 foreign teachers teach full range of courses. Negative report received from former teacher. Approach with caution.

* Hokoku Bunka Center; 920, Ishikawa-ken, Kanazawa-shi, Hondo-cho 3-2-1, MRO Bldg.; tel. 0762-22-0101. 5 foreign teachers.

* ILC; 500, Gifu, Nagasumi-cho 1-14; tel. 0582-63-3936. 2 foreign teachers.

* Ise Eigo Center; 516, Miye-ken, Iseshi, Kamihisa 1-4-11; tel. 0596-28-7629. Old but small school with only one foreign teacher on a staff of 3.

* Life Academy; 518-04, Miye-ken, Nabari-shi, Kikyogaoka 4-5-69; tel. 0595-65-0968. Features word processing training. 3 foreign teachers.

* Nagaoka Business Semmon Gakko; 940, Niigata-ken, Nagaoka-shi, Otedori 2-4-9; tel. 0258-35-1055. 2 foreign teachers.

* Yamanashi YMCA; 400, Kofu, Chuo 5-4-11; tel. 0552-35-8543. 7 foreign teachers.

* Nakamura Eigo School; 389-22, Nagano-ken; Iyama-shi, Fukuju-cho 1138; tel. 0269-62-2835. 1 foreign teacher.

* Niigata Business Semmon Gakko; 950, Niigata, Bandai 1-1-22; tel. 0252-41-2131. 6 foreign teachers.

* Nomado Gaigo Gakuin, Hattori Bldg. 3F, 3-2 Koyamachi, Shizuoka 420; tel. 0542-55-8858. All foreign teachers (5).

* YMCA Gakuin: 670, Hyogo-ken, Himeji-shi, Tsuchiyama, Higashi No-cho 9-15; tel. 0792-98-5566. 2 foreign teachers.

## OSAKA AREA ("06" dialing area)

* Abeno English/Math School; Hariake 11-59, Abeno-ku, Osaka; tel. 653-5753.
* Abeno YMCA, Minami Kawabori 9, Tennoji-ku, Osaka 543; tel. 779-8361.
* Access Systems; Umeda 1-1, Kita-ku, Osaka; tel. 343-2921.
* Ace English School; Urabae 4-21, Joto-ku, Osaka; tel. 939-2371.
* ACLA; Nakazaki Nishi 2-2, Kita-ku, Osaka; tel. 314-2267.
* Akashiya English Center; Nishi Tenman 3-5, Kita-ku, Osaka; tel. 365-8468.
* Akatsuka English School; Maruyama 1-1, Abeno-ku, Osaka; tel. 652-3399.
* ALI Iwai Beigo Gakkan, Kanaoka 3-20, Higashi Osaka 577; tel. 720-3468.
* Ambic Eikaiwa School, Dai Yuji 8, Kita-ku, Osaka 530; tel. 315-1601.
* Ambic; Nanba Sennichimae 15, Minami-ku, Osaka; tel. 644-6734.
* American English School, Higashi Sangoku 1-32, Yodogawa-ku, Osaka 532; tel. 395-3009.
* Asahi Cultural Center; Nakanoshima 3-2, Kita-ku, Osaka, ; tel. 222-5222.
* AZ English School; Dairyo 4-4, Sumiyoshi-ku, Osaka, tel. 692-0034.
* Babel Gakuin; 530, Osaka, Kita-ku, Umeda 1-11-4, Osaka Ekimae Bldg.; tel. 344-5111. 3 foreign teachers.
* Babel: Higashi Tenman 1-9, Kita-ku, Osaka; tel. 354-2079.
* Beacon Language Center; Hon 3-12, Higashi-ku, Osaka, tel. 943-8991.
* Berlitz School, Hotel Hanshin Bldg. 2F, 2-3-24 Umeda, Kita-ku, Osaka 530; tel. 341-2531.
* Berlitz; Hon 2-5, Higashi-ku, Osaka; tel. 271-4662.
* Berlitz; Kita-ku, Osaka ; tel. 311-5631.

* Bilingual Osaka; 520, Osaka, Kita-ku, Sonezaki Shinji 2-3-4, Ekimae Bldg.; tel. 344-1720. 170 foreign instructors in Bilingual chain.

* Bishop English School, 1-19 Higashi Noda, Toshima-ku, Osaka; tel. 353-6798.

* Chiari English Kenkyukai; Nishi Tenman 4-11, Kita-ku, Osaka; tel. 363-0361.

* Chiari; Denpo 2-13, Konohana-ku, Osaka; tel. 463-3737.

* Cultural Communication Int'l; Nishi Nakajima 7, Yodogawa-ku, Osaka; tel. 305-4633.

* EBJ; Denpo 1-1, Konohana-ku, Osaka; tel. 468-8638.

* ECC Gaigo Gakkoo, 2-9 Higashi Noda, Toshima-ku, Osaka 530-91; tel. 358-5904.

* ECC Osaka Gaigo Gakuin, 3-4 Shinchi, Sonezaki, Kita-ku, Osaka 530; tel. 341-6759.

* ECC; 530, Osaka, Nakazaki Nishi 2-3-35; tel. 373-0144.

* ECC; Abeno 1-6, Abeno-ku, Osaka; tel. 649-0731.

* ECC; Higashi Saka, Ashikaga 2-22, Higashi Osaka-shi, Osaka; tel. 729-5518.

* ECC; Jusanbon 1-5, Yodogawa-ku, Osaka; tel. 309-5235.

* ECC; Nanba 4-5, Minami-ku, ; tel. 633-7197.

* ECC; Umeda 2-2, Kita-ku, Osaka; tel. 341-3287.

* Echo Gaigo Gakuin, 2-1 Niimori, Asahi-ku, Osaka 535; tel. 955-1109.

* ECP Eigo Kyoiku Center, 1-17 Minami Kishibe, Suita-shi, Osaka 564; tel. 383-8691.

* Ekumi Eikaiwa School, 1-71 Naka Sonezaki, Kita-ku, Osaka 530; tel. 312-7545.

* El Business Gakko; 556, Osaka, Naniwa-ku, Nanba-naka 3-13-1; tel. 647-0011. 10 foreign teachers with hotel and tour guide classes.

* EM Gaigo Kenkyujo, 12-1 Hashizume, Uchihon-cho, Higashi-ku, Osaka 594; tel. 941-0134.

* English Academy; Shimanouchi 1-18, Minami-ku, Osaka; tel. 252-7316.

* English Academy, 1-40 Nishi Senriyama, Suita-shi, Osaka 565; tel. 385-6555.
* English Academy, 2-8 Higashi Noda, Toshima-ku, Osaka 530-91; tel. 351-6833.
* English Baret School; Imabuku Minami 2-12, Joto-ku, Osaka; tel. 393-5458.
* English Group, 2-12 Nakahama, Joto-ku, Osaka 530; tel. 962-4812.
* English Space Academy; Sonezaki Shinchi 2-3, Kita-ku, Osaka; tel. 341-6460.
* English World, 1-5 Higashi Awashi, Higashi Yodogawa-ku, Osaka 533; tel. 325-3431.
* ESO; Asahi 1-1, Abeno-ku, Osaka; tel. 649-2209.
* Esu English/Math School; Tezukayama 1-8, Abeno-ku, Osaka; tel. 653-0818.
* Esu Gakuin; Fukada 1-2, Kita-ku, Osaka; tel. 371-3069.
* Executive Gogaku Center; Nomura Bldg., 4-4-1 Hommachi, Higashi-ku, Osaka 541; tel. 271-8978. 109 foreign teachers in Executive chain.
* Foreign Language Center; Nishikiyosui 8, Minami-ku, Osaka; tel. 242-1741.
* Gloria American Center; Shincho 1-3, Nishi-ku, Osaka; tel. 538-3091.
* Gogaku Foreign Language Center; Shibada 1-4, Kita-ku, Osaka; tel. 374-0615.
* Harrow Center; 532, Osaka, Yodogawa-ku, Nishi Nakajima 3-20-8, Shinwa Bldg. 5F; tel. 428-6241. All foreign teachers (10).
* Honmachi Academy; Hon 2-5, Higashi-ku, Osaka; tel. 262-3957.
* IEC Eigo Gakuin, 4-6 Higashi Nagai, Sumiyoshi-ku, Osaka 558; tel. 696-3656.
* IF; 532, Osaka, Yodogawa-ku, Nishi Nakajima 1-9-20, Shin Nakashima Bldg. 7F; tel. 305-0721. 7 foreign teachers specialize in TOEFL/GMAT preparation.
* Ikuji Sunroom; Kamimasa Kakuji 4-5, Hirano-ku, Osaka; tel. 793-8124.
* Ikuno Foreign Language School; Shariji 3-15, Ikuno-ku, Osaka; tel. 741-8641.

* ILC; 530, Osaka, Kita-ku, Sumida-cho 8-47, Hankyu Grand Bldg. 24F; tel. 315-8003. All foreign teachers (15). Main office in London.
* Institue of Foreign Study, 1-9 Nishi Nakajima, Yodogawa-ku, Osaka 532; tel. 305-3022.
* International Academy; Nanba 1-18, Naniwa-ku, Osaka; tel. 647-2331.
* Interworld Center; Naka Hon 2-7, Higashi-ku, Osaka; tel. 943-8991.
* James Language School; Tezukayama 1-23, Abeno-ku, Osaka; tel. 654-1600.
* James Language Service Eikaiwa, Togano 15, Kita-ku, Osaka 530; tel. 315-8200.
* Junior English Center; Sogashi Higashi 3-1, Sumiyoshi-ku, Osaka; tel. 692-3847.
* Jusan Academy; Juso Higashi 2-2, Yodogawa-ku, Osaka; tel. 303-3538.
* Kansai English School, 1-27 Seigakuhon, Settsu-shi, Osaka 564; tel. 382-6276.
* KEC; 573, Osaka-fu, Hirakata-shi, Nishi Kiino 2-4-17, Daigo Matsuba Bldg.; tel. 0720-31-0616. 2 foreign teachers.
* Ken's Way; Tsukaguchi 1-21, Amagasaki-shi, Osaka; tel. 421-3513.
* Ken's Way; Tsuneyoshi Akada 1, Amagasaki-shi, Osaka; tel. 432-4474.
* Kinazu Eikaiwa, Shinko 3-9, Yodogawa-ku, Osaka 532; tel. 393-4461.
* Kingston Eikaiwa Gakuin, Nishi Nakajima 1-12, Yodogawa-ku, Osaka 532; tel. 304-0030.
* Kori Gaikokugo Center; 572, Osaka-fu, Neagawa-shi, Kori Nishino-cho 12-1; tel. 0720-31-0616. 3 foreign teachers.
* Kuji Stewardess School; Nakazaki Nishi 2-2, Kita-ku, Osaka; tel. 361-3341.
* Maria Foreign Language Gakuin; Takakonoso 4-30, Amagasaki-shi, Osaka; tel. 433-2829.
* MEC; Nakano 4-12, Higashi Sumiyoshi-ku, Osaka; tel. 797-5757.
* Minami Moricho English School; Minami Mori 2-1, Kita-ku, Osaka; tel. 364-7307.

* Momoyama English Seminar; Showa 3-1, Abeno-ku, Osaka; tel. 621-0801.

* Nakamura Kyoshitsu; Minami Sumiyoshi 3-1, Sumiyoshi-ku, Osaka; tel. 695-5133.

* Nakayama English School; Sotojima 2-9, Moriguchi-shi, Osaka; tel. 991-4077.

* Nanba Foreign Language Center; Nanba Naka 2-8, Naniwa-ku, Osaka; tel. 633-1620.

* Naniwa Foreign Language Gakuin; Nagai Higashi 4-13, Sumiyoshi-ku, Osaka; tel. 697-1958.

* Naniwa Foreign Language School; Oimasato 3-16, Higashi Nari-ku, Osaka; tel. 975-1948.

* Naniwa Foreign Lang. School; Toyosato 5-11, Higashi Yodogawa-ku, Osaka; tel. 326-5758.

* Naniwa Foreign Language School; Kiren 2-7, Hirano-ku, Osaka; tel. 708-7288.

* Naniwa Gaigo Gakuin, 7-9 Takatsu-cho, Minamai-ku, Osaka 542; tel. 641-5678.

* Naniwa School; Higashi Saka, Tsurike Moto 1-15, Higashi Osaka-shi, Osaka; tel. 745-6128.

* National LL School; Umeda 1-3, Kita-ku, Osaka; tel. 345-1272.

* NCB Eikaiwa Kyoshujo, Umeda 1-2, Kita-ku, Osaka 530; tel. 345-5111/7111.

* Nichibei English School; Umeda 1-11, Kita-ku, Osaka; tel. 344-7702.

* Nichibei English School; Nanba 1-4, Minami-ku, Osaka; tel. 211-2032.

* Nichibei Enlish School; Asahi 1-1, Abeno-ku, Osaka; tel. 649-5039.

* Nichibei Tennojiko; Abenosuji 1-5, Abeno-ku, Osaka; tel. 631-7023.

* Nihon Business School, Miahara 4-4-65, Yodogawa-ku, Osaka 532; tel. 391-0061. 4 foreign teachers.

* Nippon Eikaiwa Gakuin, Sumida 1, Kita-ku, Osaka 530; tel. 312-3730/3667/3739.

* Osaka Eigo Academy, 3-7 Tenjinbashi, Kita-ku, Osaka 530; tel. 354-1735.

* Osaka Eigo Gakkoo, 3-3 Kita-Horimachi, Tennojiku, Osaka 543; tel. 771-7659. Stresses "free conversation practice.".

* Osaka Eikaiwa Gakkoo; 530, Osaka, Kita-ku, Nakanoshima 3-6, Osaka Bldg.; tel. 441-9035. 4 foreign teachers.

* Osaka English Gakuin; Shigeta Omiya 4-2, Tsurumi-ku, Osaka; tel. 911-5680.

* Osaka Furitsu Boeki Semmon Gakko; 543, Osaka, Tennojiku, Yuhigaoka-cho 5; tel. 942-2717. 2 foreign teachers.

* Osaka Gaigo Semmon Gakko; 540, Osaka, Higashi-ku, Shimamachi 2-5; tel. 944-1061. 17 foreign teachers.

* Osaka YMCA College; 550, Osaka, Nishi-ku, Tosabori 1-5-6; tel. 441-0892. 13 foreign teachers. Mostly tour guide and hotel classes.

* Osaka YMCA Gogaku Semmon Gakkoo, 1-4-13 Sonezaki Shinchi, Kita-ku, Osaka 550; tel. 341-1701. Stresses public speaking and discussion.

* PL Foreign Language Gakuin; Shinsaibashi 1-48, Minami-ku, Osaka; tel. 241-9325.

* Rawhide English School; Minami Horie 1-11, Nishi-ku, Osaka; tel. 531-6340.

* Resta Language School, 2-1 Dojima, Kita-ku, Osaka 530; tel. 344-2062/5131.

* Sankei International College, Sankei Bldg. 8F, Umeda 2-4-9, Kita-ku, Osaka 530; tel. 347-0751. 8 foreign teachers.

* SDA, 1-40 Tani, Higashi-ku, Osaka 540; tel. 941-1107.

* Semmon Gakko Tennoji Eigo Gakuin; 545; Osaka, Abeno-ku, Matsuzaki-cho 2-9-36; tel. 623-1851. 11 foreign teachers. Recommended.

* Shibata Gakuin; Hama 1-1, Tsurumi-ku, Osaka; tel. 912-1838.

* Shin Nippon English School; Kita Sumiya 15, Minami-ku, Osaka; tel. 245-8090.

* Shogakkan Home English Center; Shibata 1-4, Kita-ku, Osaka; tel. 374-2371.

* Showa Esu Gakuin; Hanan 3-10, Abeno-ku, Osaka; tel. 623-4398.

* So English Kyoshitsu; Fuminosato 4-1, Abeno-ku, Osaka; tel. 628-2348.

* Sone English Club; Toyonaka Hama 1-4, Settsu-shi, Osaka; tel. 334-5960.

* Sony LL, Nishi Hankyu Bldg. 4F, Shibata 2-1-18, Kita-ku, Osaka 530; tel. 372-6777.

* Takakonoso English Gakuin; Takeko 1-28, Amagasaki-shi, Osaka; tel. 437-1548.

* Tennoji English Gakuin; Daido 3-1, Tennoji-ku, Osaka; tel. 771-1882.

* Tennoji English/Math Gakuin; Horikoshi 10, Tennoji-ku, Osaka; tel. 771-4609.

* Tezukayama English Center, 3-8 Tezukaya-manaka, Sumiyoshi-ku, Osaka 558; tel. 678-2548/672-5720.

* Tokyo Foreign Language Center; Chaya 18, Kita-ku, Osaka; tel. 375-0361.

* Tomo English School; 530, Osaka, Kita-ku, Doshin 2-2-15, Sun Laurel 301; tel. 352-0687. 3 foreign teachers.

* Tsurugaoka Eigo Club, 5-2 Yamazaka, Higashi Sumiyoshi-ku, Osaka 546; tel. 696-3934.

* Uehara English Juku; Hanan 5-18, Abeno-ku, Osaka; tel. 623-7584.

* ULS English Kyoshitsu; Hanan 3-14, Abeno-ku, Osaka; tel. 623-2190.

* Umeda Gakuin Eigo Semmon Gakkoo, 2-30 Chayayamachi, Kita-ku, Osaka 530; tel. 376-0661. Mostly adult students for 11 foreign teachers.

* Universal Gaigo Gakuin, 2-39 Azuchi, Higashi-ku, Osaka 541; tel. 266-0395.

* World English Juku; Nishi Kawanomoto 1-61, Amagasaki-shi, Osaka; tel. 499-7119.

* World Language School; Umeda 1-3, Kita-ku, Osaka; tel. 341-6636.

* Yamatani English Gakuin; Takekonoso 1-3, Amagasaki-shi, Osaka; tel. 436-0685.

* YMCA Telephone Service; Takashima 1-5, Kita-ku, Osaka; tel. 341-2315.

* YMCA; Higashi Saka, Mishiku Minami 3-1, Higashi Osaka-shi, Osaka; tel. 787-3232.

* Yomiuri Gaigo Business Semmon, 2-5 Shima, Higashi-ku, Osaka 540; tel. 944-1091.

* Yotsubashi English School; Kita Horie 1-10, Nishi-ku, Osaka; tel. 538-3096.
* YSF Eigo Kyoshitsu, Omiya 5-2, Asahi-ku, Osaka 535; tel. 953-8665.
* YWCA Secretarial Arts School; 550, Osaka, Kita-ku, Kamiyama-cho 11-12; tel. 361-0838. 8 foreign teachers.

KYOTO AREA

* Bilingual English Conversation School; 605 Kyoto, Higashiyama-ku, Shijodori, Yamato-oji Nishi Iru, Nakanomachi 200, Kamogawa Bldg. 9F. "An expanding company" which has found JOBS IN JAPAN "valuable in that it has led many prospective teachers to our doorstep for interviews." .
* ECC; 604, Kyoto, Nakagyo-ku, Karawamachi-dori, Shijo Agaru; tel. 075-223-0196.
* Kyoto English Center, Sumitomo Seimei Bldg. 8F, Nishi Shijo Karasuma, Shimo Nyooku, Kyoto 600; tel. 075-221-2251. Emphasizes extra-curricular activities with students and foreign teachers (45).
* Kyoto YMCA, Kado, Sanjo Yanagibajo, Nakagyo-ku, Kyoto 604; tel. 075-231-4388. Together with next listing, 50 foreign teachers.
* Kyoto YMCA Semmon Gakkoo, Sagaru, Imadegawa Karasuma, Kamigyoku, Kyoto 602; tel. 075-432-3191. Emphasizes practical business skills.
* Lake Gaigo Gakuin, Ikawa Hairu, Higashi Horikawa, Nakagyoku, Kyoto 604; tel. 075-221-7686. Conversation stressed for 10 foreign teachers.
* Nara Gaigo Business Typist Gakuin; 634, Nara-ken, Kashihara-shi, Uchizen-cho 5-3-31, Fuji Bldg. 7F; tel. 0744-22-7688. 3 foreign teachers.
* Riseikan Gaikuin; 663, Hyogo-ken, Nishinomiya-shi, Kitaguchi-cho 4-25; tel. 0798-65-2011. 8 foreign teachers.
* SEI; 520, Shiga-ken, Otsu-shi, Kyomachi 3-2-6, Eiki Bldg. 3F; tel. 0775-24-8879. 2 foreign teachers.

## KOBE AREA *("078" dialing area)*

* Anbik Gaigo Gakuin, Ikuta-ku, Kobe 650; tel. 331-1561.
* Berlitz, Kyowa Bldg. 4F, 5-12-7 Shimoyamate-dori,, Chuo-ku, Kobe 650; tel. 351-1583.
* Clara Gaigo School, 1-39 Nakayamate, Ikuta-ku, Kyoto 650; tel. 241-3288.
* ECC, 1-1-1 Nishi Tachibanadori, Hyogo-ku, Kobe 652; tel. 576-7758. 4 foreign teachers. See description of ECC earlier.
* ECC, Sannomiya 1-17, Ikuta-ku, Kobe 650; tel. 321-2419.
* Executive School, Shokoboeki Center Bldg., 5-1-14, Hamabedori, Chuo, Kobe 651; tel. 251-2412. See description of Executive earlier.
* Kobe YMCA, 2-7-15 Kanocho, Chuo-ku, Kobe 650; tel. 241-7201. 5 foreign teachers. See description of YMCA earlier.
* Kokusai Business Gakuin, 5-3-5 Kotono Ocho, Chuo-ku, Kobe 651; tel. 242-5178. Training for business/ industry. 2 foreign teachers.
* KS Eikaiwa, 3-9-7 Sannomiya-cho, Chuo-ku, Kobe 650; tel. 391-8711; tel. 391-8711. "KS" stands for "kindness and sincerity." (Really, I don't make this stuff up.)
* Seinikaeru Kokusai Gakkoo, 3-17-2 Nakayamate-dori, Chuo-ku, Kobe 650; tel. 221-8028. Trains students for Cambridge. 5 British instructors.
* Toa Gaigo Gakuin, Ikuta-ku, Kobe 650; tel. 321-2339.

## NAGOYA

* Asahi Culture Center; 460, Aichi-ken, Nagoya, Naka-ku, Sakae 3-4-5, Marue Sky 10F; tel. 052-261-3866. 2 foreign teachers.
* Nagoya Business Semmon Gakko, Denba 3-2-3, Atsuta-ku, Nagoya 456; tel. 052-682-7879. 3 foreign students.

* Nagoya Gaikokugo Semmon Gakkoo; Imaike 1-5-31, Chikusaku, Nagoya 464; tel. 741-2304. 20 foreign teachers teach mostly business classes.
* Nagoya International School, 2686 Minamihara, Nakashidami, Moriyama-ku, Nago-ya 463. Not an ESL school. Generally hires only experienced instructors with teaching credentials to teach general junior and high school curriculum.
* Nihon Business School, Mei Eki Minami 1-23-17, Nakamura-ku, Nagoya 450; tel. 582-3026. 5 foreign teachers.
* Professional English Course; 461, Aichi-ken, Nagoya, Higashi-ku, Aori 1-25-1, Nishin Bldg. 508; tel. 052-937-7339. 10 foreign teachers.

## SHIKOKU ISLAND

* Anbik School; 770, Tokushima, Terashima Hon-cho, Nishi Ichome, Awa Kendo Bldg. 5F; tel. 0886-25-4291. 5 foreign teachers.
* Ehime Eigo Academy, 2-9-6 Ichiban-cho, Matsuyama-shi, Ehime-ken 790; tel. 0899-31-8686. 7 foreign teachers.
* Takamatsu Nichibei Gakuin, 10-20 Marunouchi, Takamatsu-shi, Kagawa-ken 760; tel. 0878-21-3382. 5 foreign teachers.

## FUKUOKA AND SOUTHERN JAPAN

* American Center; 880, Miyazaki, Hachiba-na-dori Higashi 5-3, Ono Bldg. 3F; tel. 0985-53-4521. 2 foreign teachers feature role play and public speaking.
* Berlitz, Futaba Bldg. 7F, Tenjin 3-1, Chuo-ku, Fukuoka, 810; tel. 751-9888. See Berlitz description earlier.
* Caine's Eikaiwa Typing School, 1-1 Maizuru, Chuo-ku, Fukuoka 810; tel. 721-5020. 14 foreign teachers for business, vocational and general classes.

* ECC Gaigo Gakuin; 810, Fukuoka, Chuo-ku, Daimyo 2-9-5; tel. 092-715-0731. See ECC description earlier.

* ELC; 880, Miyazaki, Miyata-cho 10-22, Eikaiwa Bldg. 2F; tel. 0985-25-1565. 3 foreign teachers. Many types of classes.

* Hiroshima YMCA; 730, Hiroshima, Naka-ku, Hachobori 7-11; tel. 082-228-2269. 9 foreign teachers.

* Kagoshima Foreign Language Center, Dai Ichi Seimei Bldg. Zenkan, 4-1 Oguro-cho, Kagoshima 892; tel. 0992-23-6824. 3 foreign teachers.

* Kitakyushu YMCA; 802, Fukuoka-ken, Kitakyushu-shi, Kokura Kita-ku, Kaji-cho 2-3-13; tel. 093-531-1587. 4 foreign teachers with variety of courses.

* Kumamoto YMCA; 860, Kumamoto, Shinmachi 1-3-8; tel. 096-353-6391. 8 foreign teachers for general classes.

* Nihon Business School; 812, Fukuoka, Hakata Ekimae 4-18-6; tel. 092-411-6423. 3 foreign teachers, mostly vocational English classes.

* Okinawa English Center; 900, Okinawa-ken, Naha-shi, Izumizaki 1-11-12; tel. 0988-61-1487. 3 foreign instructor. Okinawa is an island about 500 miles from the mainland.

* Sato Business School, 2-4-10 Tenjin, Chuo-ku, Fukuoka 810; tel. 771-8261. 4 foreign instructors.

* SDA; 730, Hiroshima, Naka-ku, Takeya-cho 4-8; tel. 082-241-2464. All foreign teachers (4).

## SAPPORO AND NORTHERN JAPAN

* Akita Eikaiwa School; 010, Akita, Nakadori 3-1-9, Kanda Bldg.; tel. 0188-33-4843. 2 foreign teachers in small school.

* IAY; 060, Sapporo, Chuo-ku, Minami Ichijo 4-chome, Hinode Bldg.; tel. 011-281-5188. 19 foreign teachers. Large school with wide variety of classes.

* Berlitz, Sapporo Bldg. 9F, Nihon Seimei, 4-1-1 Nishi, Kita Sanjo, Chuo-ku, Sapporo 060; tel.

221-4701. All foreign teachers (11). See earlier description of Berlitz.

* English Circles/EC; 060, Sapporo, Chuo-ku, Minami Ichijo Nishi 5-chome, President Bldg. 3F; tel. 011-221-0279. 10 foreign teachers in Sapporo's largest and oldest English school.

* Fukushima Eigo Gakuin, 9-29 Moriai-cho, Fukushima 960; tel. 0245-35-5670. Primarily grade school and junior high school-age students. 1 foreign teacher.

* James Eikaiwa; 980, Miyage-ken, Sendai-shi, Chuo 3-3-10, Chuo Sogo Bldg. 5F; tel. 0222-67-4911. All foreign teachers (19) for general classes.

* New Day School; 980, Sendai-shi, Kokubu-cho 2-15-16, Company Bldg. 5F; tel. 0222-65-4288. 16 foreign teachers specialize in children's classes.

* Nihon Business School; 001, Sapporo, Kita-ku, Kita Rokujo Nishi 6-chome; tel. 011-717-7751. 4 foreign teachers. Emphasis on vocational English.

* Nihon Business School; 980, Sendai-shi, Higashi Kyuban-cho 122; tel. 0222-99-1641. 1 foreign teacher.

* Nihon Business Sogo Semmon Gakuin; 060, Sapporo, Chuo-ku, Odori Higashi 1, Odori Bus Center Bldg.; tel. 011-241-8311. 5 foreign teacher. Vocational English classes offered primarily.

* Tohoku Gaikokugo Gakkoo, Chuo 4-2-25, Sendai-shi, Miagi-ken 980; tel. 0222-67-3847. 13 foreign teachers emphasizes conversation for vocational training.

## ENGLISH SCHOOLS IN KOREA

The following is a list of private language schools in the two largest cities in Korea (Seoul and Pusan). When writing, spell out "FLI" as "Foreign Language Institute" and print the address clearly. Generally, the larger the school, the greater its need for foreign teachers. Size of the school may be judged by the number of students noted in parentheses at the end of each listing (when available). "Recommended" schools have been favorably mentioned by local teachers.

SEOUL AREA *("02" telephone prefix)*

* Asia Foreign Language Institute, Socho-ku, Banpo-dong, Kangnam; tel. 549-1536/5117.
* Baeyoung FLI, 1513-2 Sinlim-dong, Kwanak-ku; tel. 878-9490. (120 students)
* BCM (English Educational Center), Socho 1318-8, Kangnam-yok; tel. 569-3161.
* BCM (English Educational Center), Songpa; tel. 412-2335.
* Central Language Institute/CLI (Chung-ang FLI), So-cho 1318-1; tel. 556-9944.
* Central Language Institute/CLI (Chung-ang FLI), Namhyun 1062-15; tel. 588-8555.
* Chongro FLI, 55 Kongpyung-dong, Chongro-ku; tel. 732-8381. (280)
* Choongbu Daewon FLI, 290 Changshin-dong, Chung-ku; tel. 744-4290. (190)
* Daeil FLI, 907-11, Sinjung-dong, Yangchon-ku; tel. 690-3885. (680)
* Daeil FLI, 1570-1 Sinlim 11-dong, Kwanak-ku; tel. 855-6343. (295)
* Daelim FLI, 413-80 Kuro-dong, Kuro-ku; tel. 853-0708. (240)
* Daenak FLI, 134-2 Youngdeungpo-dong 4 ka; tel. 678-5501. (160)
* Daesung FLI, 139-15 Garibong-dong, Kuro-ku; tel. 862-3963. (250)

* Daewon FLI, 72-16 Noryangjin-dong, Dongjak-ku; tel. 814-2227. (200)
* Daeyang FLI, 406-1 Poongnap-dong, Songpa-ku; tel. 467-0408.
* Dongbu FLI, 439-13 Sungnae-dong, Kangdong-ku; tel. 475-0700. (432)
* Dongil FLI, 11-33 Dangsan-dong 5 ka, Youngdeungpo-ku; tel. 679-8606. (304)
* Dongsoong FLI, 1-5 Dongsoong-dong, Chongro-ku; tel. 763-0226. (1290)
* Dongwoo FLI, 3Fl Jangmi Sangka, 40 Yoido-dong, Youngdeungpo-ku; tel. 783-0648. (240)
* ECC Language School, Chongro 2-55-1; tel. 277-6812. (Recommended)
* Elite FLI, 140-29 Garibong-dong, Kruo-ku; tel. 865-0916. (210)
* ELS/ Kangbuk Sisa FLI , 2-55-1 Chongro, Chongro-ku; tel. 278-2902/5. (230) (Recommended)
* Hanguk FLI, Kwanchol 15-1; tel. 732-0601. (Recommended)
* Hanil FLI, 5Fl Dukeui B/D, 53-12 Yoido-dong, Youngdeungpo-ku; tel. 782-9049. (260)
* Hanil FLI, 67-5 Sungnae-dong, Kangdong-ku; tel. 483-9439. (280)
* Hankuk FLI, 15-1 Kwanchul-dong, Chongro-ku; tel. 734-7329. (280)
* Hanlim FLI, Nam Seoul B/D, 20-2 Youngdeung-dong 4 ka; tel. 678-6426. (220)
* Hyundae Sisa FLI, 5-3 Kwanchul-dong, Chongro-ku; tel. 273-4395.
* Hyundai English School, 189 Choongjungro 3 ka, Seodaemun-ku; tel. 353-3291. (80)
* Hyundai FLI, 1021-9 Sinjung-dong, Yangchon-ku; tel. 648-7789. (720)
* Hyundai FLI, 188-40 Sando-dong, Dongjak-ku; tel. 841-6774. (100)
* Hyundai FLI, Suktae, Namyoung-dong; tel. 703-0005/0055.
* Hyundai Interpreting School, 69-3 Kalweol-dong, Yongsan-ku; tel. 715-0555. (2730)
* Jamsil FLI, 7 Sincheon-dong, Songpa-ku; tel. 414-9319. (160)

* Jeil FLI, 14, 15 Karak Jiku 64 B/D, Songpa-ku; tel. 407-1125. (712)

* Jongchol FLI, Kangnam-yok; tel. 553-9911.

* Jong Ro FLI, 55 Kong Pyung-dong, Jongro-ku; tel. 732-8383/734-0114. (Recommended)

* Joongwon FLI, 163-2, Heuksuk-dong, Dongjak-ku; tel. 814-4953. (200)

* Kana FLI, 862-2, Bongchon-dong, Kwanak-ku; tel. 887-0505. (120)

* Kangsuh Jeil FLI, 275-3 Yumchang-dong, Kangsu-ku; tel. 694-2986. (336)

* Korea FLI, 16-1 Kwanchul-dong, Chongro-ku; tel. 739-6000. (110)

* Korea Herald FLI, 65-1 Suha-dong, Chung-ku; tel. 757-0419. (2520) (Recommended)

* Koryo FLI, 2-9 Chongro, Chongro-ku; tel. 739-8000. (Credible complaint received; approach with caution.)

* Kukdong FLI, 334-1 Kunja-dong, Sungdong-ku; tel. 243-6928. (600)

* Kukje FLI (ILI), Tangju 16-1; tel. 735-3535.

* Kukje FLI, 5-76 Changjung-dong, Mapokku; tel. 338-2244. (400)

* Kukje FLI, 2-103-3 Hankangro, Yongsan-ku. (120)

* Kukje FLI, Noryangjin 54-7, Dongjak-ku; tel. 813-5522. (90)

* Kumkang FLI, Satang 3-23-1; tel. 536-9457

* (Kwanyin) Chinjin Language Institute, So-cho 1667-13; tel. 521-3337.

* (Kwanyin) Kojun FLI, Ap-ku, Chong Yok Sakori; tel. 548-4254.

* Kyunghee, Nam Seoul B/D, 20-2 Youngdeung-dong 4 ka; tel. 678-1221. (540)

* Kyungki FLI, 454-7 Karak-dong, Songpa-ku; tel. 424-2480. (160)

* Kyungwon FLI, 1125-2, Kuro 3-dong, Kuro-ku; tel. 868-3300. (500)

* Language Education School, 1-60-17 Taepyungro, Chung-ku; tel. 738-0709. (280)

* LTRC (Chedan FLI), Taepyung-ro 1-60-17, tel. 737-4641.

* Misung FLI, 1655 Sinlim 8-dong, Kwanak-ku; tel. 853-4629. (120)
* Monnwa FLI, 182-2 Jamsil Bon-dong, Songpa-ku; tel. 422-4151. (252)
* Munwha FLI, 2-88-2 Euljiro, Chung-ku; tel. 267-3569. (480)
* Nambu FLI, 151-10 Noryangjin-dong, Dongjak-ku; tel. 815-7819. (360)
* Namsung FLI, 155-2 Sadang-dong, Dongjak-ku; tel. 591-4512. (180)
* New Hankuk, Youngchang B/D, 54-6, Yoido-dong, Youngdeungpo-ku; tel. 784-2607/8. (300)
* New Kukje FLI, 16-1 Kangju-dong, Chongro-ku. (370)
* Nam Seoul FLI, Sinsa 600-5; tel. 515-7333.
* New Seoul FLI, 67 Youngdeungpo-dong, 4 ka; tel. 678-5537. (425)
* New York FLI, 457-4 Kil-dong, Songpa-ku; tel. 478-4124. (292)
* Oryun FLI, 15-2 Songpa-dong, Song-pa-ku; tel. 417-7219. (256)
* Pagoda FLI, Chongro 2-56-6; tel. 277-8257, 275-9880, 274-4000. (290) (Recommended)
* Plaza FLI, Taepyung-ro 2-69-15; tel. 778-5000.
* Saekuru FLI, Satang 3-324-16; tel. 535-0503.
* Samsung FLI, 862-2 Bongchon-dong, Kwanak-ku; tel. 877-7137. (160)
* Samwon FLI, 415-8 Sungnae-dong, Kangdong-ku; tel. 487-2236. (162)
* Samyuk FLI, 287-1 Hwikyung-dong, Dongdaemun-ku; tel. 244-7521. (1800)
* Samyuk FLI, 339-1, Daebang-dong, Dongjak-ku; tel. 812-8931. (1080)
* Sangdo Hyundae FLI, Sangdo 188-40; tel. 822-5525.
* SDA Sam-yuk FLI, Hui-kyung 287-1; tel. 244-1275. Affiliated with Seventh Day Adventist Church (Recommended)
* Sejong FLI, 1433-45 Sinlim-dong, Kwanak-ku; tel. 877-4422. (150)

* Seoul FLI, 5Fl Yoochang B/C, 46-1 Yoido-dong, Youngdeungpo-ku; tel. 783-4511. (748)

* Seoul FLI, 322Ho, B Sangka, Jamsil 6-dong, Songpa-ku; tel. 422-5604. (210)

* Seoul Haewei FLI, 544-1 Kuro-dong, Kuro-ku; tel. 856-5911. (420)

* Seoul Tong Yok Translation School; tel. 717-7009/10.

* Shinchon FLI, Taehyun 40-4; tel. 392-0994.

* Silyong FLI, 1006 Paiksang B/D, 35-2 Yoido-dong, Youngdeungpo-ku; tel. 785-1749. (493)

* Sisa English Institute, Kwangchol 19-23, Chongro-ku; tel. 732-6329/734-2442. (780) (Recommended)

* Sisa FLI, 3Fl Youngsin sangka 18, Youngdeunpo-dong 5 ka; tel. 634-1265. (190)

* Songpa FLI, 84-7 Songpa-dong, Songpa-ku; tel. 419-2912. (768)

* Soodo FLI, 7-1 Kangsan-dong 1 ka, Youngdeungpo-ku; tel. 678-1999. (200)

* Sudo FLI, Sung-in 1063; tel. 922-9861.

* Suhjung FLI, 621-24 Banghwa-dong, Kangsu-ku; tel. 663-4577. (360)

* Sunjin FLI, 411-13 Okum-dong, Songpa-ku; tel. 406-5300. (299)

* Sungmin FLI, 139-5 Youngdeungpo-dong 1 ka; tel. 679-0066. (580)

* Sungsuh FLI, 47-9 Songpa-dong, Songpa-ku; tel. 416-8911. (180)

* Sunkwang FLI, 1042 Doksan 2-dong, Kuro-ku; tel. 805-5383. (126)

* Trust FLI, Dongja-dong, Yongsan-ku 43-59; tel. 702-6737. (236)

* Ungji FLI, Myung-il 324-1; tel. 479-0075.

* Yeil FLI, Elite B/C 44-32 Yoido-dong, Youngdeungpo-ku; tel. 783-7665. (380) (Recommended)

* Yeonil FLI, 184-4 Jamsil-dong, Songpa-ku; tel. 423-3604. (170)

* YMCA FLI, Chongro 2-9; tel. 734-1161/735-4612. (640)

* Yoido FLI, 3Fl Jinjoo Sangka, 54-2
Yoido-dong, Youngdeungpo-ku; tel. 783-0596. (880)
(Recommended)
* Yoido Sisa FLI, 3Fl Jinjoo Sangka, 54-2
Yoido-dong, Youngdeungpo-ku; tel. 783-0061. (124)
* Youngche FLI, Donhyun 142-4; tel. 548-1992.
* Youngdeungpo FLI, 146 Youngdeungpo-dong;
tel. 678-3484. (250)
* Youngduk FLI, Hongwoo B/D, 43-3,
Yoido-dong, Youngdeungpo-ku; tel. 780-2451. (700)
* Youngil FLI, 52 Youngdeungpo-dong, 4 ka;
tel. 678-7098. (498)
* Youngsei FLI, 410-209 Karak-dong,
Songpa-ku; tel. 414-6778. (329)
* Yu-in FLI, Socho 1697-9; tel. 594-4844.

PUSAN *("051" telephone prefix)*

* Dong-A FLI, 505-21 Hadan-dong, Saha-ku;
tel. 206-1633. (150)
* Dongrae FLI, 266 Nakin-dong, Dongrae-ku;
tel. 554-4546. (480)
* Sisa English School, 1198-2 Chorang 5-dong,
Dong-ku; tel. 44-7424. (400)
* Epel FLI, 1740-2 Daeyeon-dong; tel. 644-3942.
(180)
* ESS FLI, 1-9-2 Shinchang-dong, Choong-ku;
tel. 23-5211/2. (900)
* Ewha FLI, 999-2 Daeyeon 4-dong. (339)
* Hankuk FLI, 271-51 Yangjung 2-dong; tel.
83-2766. (160)
* Hyundai FLI, 74-2 Daeyeon 3-dong; tel.
623-1941. (185)
* Ilyoung FLI, 154-1 Bumil-dong, Dong-ku; tel.
644-3021. (160)
* Jeil FLI, Rm. 302, Pusan Dept. 1-1
Dongkwang-dong, Choong-ku; tel. 23-8291. (40)
* Jinhak FLI, 1-20-30 Buyong-dong, Seo-ku;
tel. 242-7284. (180)
* Kuduk, 3-506 Seodaeshin-dong, Seo-ku; tel.
244-0770. (40)

* Kukje FLI, 4-31-1 Chongang-dong, Choong-ku; tel. 462-5434. (60)
* Kumsung FLI, 1436-5 Onchon-dong, Dongrae-ku; tel. 553-5401. (440)
* Kyungnam FLI, 2-42-2 Dongdaeshin-dong, Seo-ku; tel. 243-1277. (180)
* People FLI, 70-4 Keojae 1-dong, Dongrae-ku; tel. 863-2090. (440)
* Pusan FLI, 5-33 Nampo-dong, Choong-ku; tel. 22-6525. (260)
* Pusan FLI, 415-21, Jangjun 3-dong, Dongrae-ku; tel. 512-0512. (260)
* Samwoo FLI, 1-4-11 Choongmuro, Seo-ku; tel. 256-4828. (45)
* SDA Samyuk FLI, 62-7 Youngju-dong, Choong-ku; tel. 44-3536. (800)
* SDA FLI, 129-1 Bujun-dong, Jin-ku; tel. 44-3536. (1000)
* Seomyun FLI, 241-18 Bujun-dong, Jin-ku; tel. 88-3256. (288)
* Serabul FLI, 497-32 Hadan-dong, Saha-ku; tel. 205-4150. (300)
* Shinil FLI, 1949-12, Yonsan 7-dong, Dongrae-ku; tel. 862-0916. (150)
* Simbun FLI, 416-5 Jangjun 2-dong, Dongrae-ku; tel. 56-2928. (120)
* Sisa FLI, 1-21-1, Youngsun-don, Yongdo-ku; tel. 37-0707. (40)
* Sisa FLI, 6F, Hanjin Bldg., Bujun 2-dong, Jin-ku; tel. 805-0373. (280)
* SWS FLI, 257-25, Bujun-dong, Jin-ku; tel. 803-3200. (1314)
* Time FLI, 241-5, Bujun 2-dong, Jin-ku; tel. 806-0808. (140)
* Trust FLI, 4F Hyundai Bldg., 2-5 Choongang-dong, Choong-ku; tel. 22-4167/2891.
* Yeil FLI, 833-8 Bumil-dong, Dong-ku; tel. 642-5541. (120)
* YMCA FLI, 1143-138 Chorang 3-dong, Chong-ku; tel. 462-2866. (120)
* Youngnam FLI, 558-1 Quebup-dong; tel. 327-1608. (116)

## ENGLISH SCHOOLS IN TAIWAN

The following schools employ foreigners as instructors in Taiwan. Mention here is no guarantee of quality or reputability. Conferring with current foreign instructors prior to making any commitment is advised. Also contact Chinese-language schools (this Appendix) which frequently also teach conversational English.

TAIPEI AREA *("02" Dialing Code)*

* Ai-Sin Language Center, 13 Wanlin Street, Taipei; tel. 381-1551.
* American Children's School, Kechiang Road #34, Shihlien, Taipei; tel. 831-6661/16.
* American Institute, Program for Advanced English Studies, Taipei; tel. 309-1344.
* Cathay Language Center, 2F 8 Lane 190, Chungshan North Rd., Sec. 7, Tienmu, Taipei; tel. 872-9165.
* Chang-Chin English Center, 1-20 Chahsin, Lane 363, Taipei; tel. 735-2617. Also at 44 Nanking East Road, Section 1; tel. 581-2988.
* Chia-Lio Language Center, 7 Tsingtao East Road 3F; Taipei; tel. 341-9226/5.
* Chi-Dan Language Center, 386 Pateh Road 4F-1, Section 2, Taipei; tel. 772-3740.
* Chi-Wen English School, 8F, 128 Chunghsiao East Road, Taipei, tel. 711-3788/3786.
* Chia-Chi English Center, 57-2 Chungking South Road 2F, Section 2, Taipei; tel. 394-4921.
* Chen-Mei English School, 22 Kuan-Chen Road, Taipei; tel. 312-2925/6.
* Chia-Yi English School, 90 Sungkiang Road 2F, Lane 90; tel. 564-1607.
* Chia-Yin English School, 57-2 Chungking South Road, Section 2, Taipei; tel. 394-5623.
* Chih-Ren English School, 33 Chunghsiao West Road 9F, Section 1, Taipei; tel. 381-8811. Business English classes.

* China Language Institute, Lane 82, 4 An Ho Rd., Taipei; tel. 708-7157.

* Ching-Hua Language School, 312 Roosevelt 6F, Section 3, Taipei; tel. 391-7623.

* Chi-Yuan English School, 37 Chungshan North Road, Lane 50, Section 2, Taipei; tel. 551-2259. Children's classes.

* Chong-Hua Language Center, 529 Chungshan North Road 2F, Section 5, Taipei; tel. 882-1585/6. Also at 104 Hsinyi Road, Section 2; tel. 393-8805.

* Chong-Lin English Center, 603 Tunhua North Road 11F-3, Taipei; tel. 704-9268/9.

* Chunghsiao Language Center, 21-1 Chunghsian North Road, Section 2, Taipei; tel. 312-2512.

* Community Service Center, 25 Lane 290, Chungshan North Rd., Sec. 6, Tienmu, Taipei; tel. 836-8134.

* Da-Shia Language School, 3 Ningpo West Road 3F, Taipei; tel. 321-7784.

* Da-Shih-Tai English School, 41 Roosevelt Road 5F, Section 2, Taipei; tel. 351-5533. Well-known school.

* Da-Wen Language Center, 1-1 Nanking West Road 5F, Taipei; tel. 551-4630.

* Doctor English School, 24 Nan-Yang Street, Taipei; tel. 361-4673.

* Egret English Center, 109 Hoping East Road 10F, Section 1, Taipei; tel. 392-0276. North American English preferred.

* ELC English School, Chunghsiao West Road, Section 1, #72 5F, Taipei; tel. 311-4595. Very large school.

* ELSI Language School, 59 Chung King South Road, Section 2, Taipei; tel. 321-9005.

* E2 American English School, Minchuang East Road, Section 2 #42, Taipei. Mostly children's classes.

* Everyday Language Center (ELC), 72 Chunghsiao West Road 5F, Sec. 1, Taipei; tel. 311-4595.

* Fu-Chin English School, 196 Shing-Long Road, Section 2, Taipei; tel. 931-7665. North American English preferred.
* GEOS Language Systems, Chunghsiao East Road 9F, Section 4, Taipei; tel. 740-7700.
* Gran English School, Rm. 7A 402 Tunhua South Road; tel. 741-0047/0970.
* Green English School, 164 Roosevelt Road, Section 4; tel. 396-0630.
* Gren Language Center, 402 Tunhua South Road 7F, Taipei; tel. 741-0970.
* Han-Bon Language Center, 91 Chongchung Road 2F, Lane 17, Taipei; tel. 531-6777.
* Han-Chia English School, 442 Fu-Chin 1F, Taipei; tel. 766-3916.
* Han-Sheng English School, 60-8 Hoping East Road 3F, Section 2, Taipei; tel. 735-4395.
* He-Chia-Jun American English School, 146 Chungking Road, Section 3, Neihu, Taipei. Mostly children's classes.
* Ho-Chia-Jun American English School, 2 Hsinyi Road, Lane 199, Section 4, Taipei.
* Heh-Chia-Ren English Center, 49-1 Hopin East Road 3F, Section 2, Taipei; tel. 706-0464. Well-known school.
* Hess Language School, 182 Chung Cheng Road, Shih Lin, Taipei; tel. 836-6324.
* Ho-Chia-Ren English School, 333 Chonghsiao East Road, Section 4, Taipei; tel. 776-5622/3.
* Hsia-Mei English Center, 50 Fuhsing North Road 2F, Taipei; tel. 772-1022. North American English preferred.
* Hsi-Chuan Language Center, 59 Chungking South Road 2F, Taipei; tel. 312-0632.
* Hsi-Hai Language Center, 64 Jenai Road, Section 4, Taipei; tel. 704-4000.
* Hsin-Fua English School, 41 Chunghua Road 11F, Section 1, Taipei; tel. 331-4800.
* Hua-Dou English School, 20 Roosevelt Road, Section 1, Taipei; tel. 341-2519.
* Huanan English School, 6-5 Chinmen Street 6F, Lane 34, Taipei; tel. 351-4026.

* Jen-Dang Language Center, 9 Hangchou South Road, Lane 9, Section 1, Taipei; tel. 341-2694.
* Jordan English Language School, 16 Pei Ping Road 6F, Taipei; tel. 396-7581/3272.
* Jordan English Language School, 97 Chuan Gow St., Taipei; tel. 309-0863. Also 9 Jenai Road, Section 3; tel. 772-8170.
* Jason English School, 31 Der-Huey Street 2F, Taipei; tel. 591-7340.
* Kechien American English School, 9 Sungkiang Road, Lane 90, Taipei; tel. 564-3500. Also at 87 Ninpo West Road; tel. 396-7092. Well-known school.
* Keh-Chi English Center, 95 Chongchun South Road 7F, Section 1, Taipei; tel. 361-3742.
* Kid Castle American English School, Taipei; tel. 916-1758.
* Kuan-Kuang Language Center, 66 Koufeng Road 2F, Section 1, Taipei; tel. 371-6741.
* Kuo-Chi Language Center, 79 Kirin Road 4F, Taipei; tel. 561-1112.
* Kuo-Ting Language Center, 174 Nanking East Road 3F, Section 2, Taipei; tel. 541-0434.
* Lai-Hsin Language Center, 12 Nanyang Street, Taipei; tel. 314-1923/6356. Also at 42 Shichang Street 7F; tel. 381-5576.
* Lancer Language School, 1 Chih Cheng Rd., Lane 62, Alley 10, Section 1, Shih Lin, Taipei; tel. 835-5451.
* Language Training & Testing Center, 170 Chinhai Rd., Section 2, Taipei; tel. 362-6385.
* Lang-Wen English School, 16 Chin Chou Street 3F, Taipei; tel. 551-8956.
* Liang-Yu Language Center, 76-1 Chunghsiao East Road, Section 4, Taipei; tel. 741-1421.
* Marcolian English School, 122 Chunghsiao West Road 8F, Taipei; tel. 311-3411.
* Mei-Chan Language Center, 439 Pateh Road 2F, Section 2, Taipei; tel. 772-9470/35.
* Mei-Chia English Center, 40-90 Nanyoung Street, Taipei; tel. 331-8055.

* Mei-Fu English School, 23 Hsinyi Road, Section 3, Taipei; tel. 701-7579.
* Mei-Sheng Language Center, 3 Roosevelt Road, Lane 269, Section 3, Taipei; tel. 321-6281. North American English preferred.
* Mei-Ur-Dun English School, 39 Chungsan North Road, Section 3, Taipei; tel. 594-1434/0514.
* Meiya English School, 126-8 Hsinsheng South Road, Section 1, Taipei; tel. 321-7826.
* Mei-Yu Language Center, 13 Nanyoung 7F, Taipei; tel. 331-6281.
* Melton English School, 8 Chinan Road, Section 3, Taipei; tel. 771-2208.
* Merica Language School, 50 Naiyang Road, Meichia Bldg., Taipei; tel. 381-1166/389-9689. One of the largest English school in Taiwan.
* Minsheng English Center, 1114 Minsheng East Road 1F, Taipei; tel. 769-9243. North American English preferred.
* Min-Tai English School, 178 Chong-Hua Road 2F, Section 1, Taipei; tel. 311-0712.
* MY Language School, 2F 126-8 Singsheng South Road, Section 1, Taipei; tel. 321-7636.
* Republic of China (Taiwan) English Association, Taipei; tel. 731-6267, 371-8408.
* Ruei-Huan English Center, 46 Minhseng East Road 10F, Taipei; tel. 537-5015/6. North American English preferred.
* San-Der Language Center, 53 Chunghsiao West Road 5F, Section 1, Taipei; tel. 381-3721/0.
* San-Shan Language Center, 54 Chunghsiao East Road 3F, Section 4, Taipei; tel. 776-3786.
* San-Young Language School, 208 Hsinyi Road 6F, Section 2, Taipei; tel. 392-3754.
* Shi-Fong English Center, 12 Bing-An Street, Lane 4, Taipei; tel. 917-2157.
* Shi-Tai Language Center, 59 Chungking South Road 10F-2, Section 2, Taipei; tel. 341-4175. North American English preferred.
* St. John English School, 47 Chunghsiao West Rod 2F, Section 1, Taipei; tel. 381-4169.

* Ta-Cheng American English School, 24 Tong-hua Street 4F, Lane 38, Taipei; tel. 709-0739. North American English preferred.
* Taipei Language Institute, 104 Hsinyi Road 7F, Section 2, Taipei; tel. 393-8805.
* Taipei Language Institute, 238 Shih Tung Road, Shih Lin, Taipei; tel. 832-7330.
* Taipei Language Institute Group, PO Box 91-225, Taipei; tel. 362-9573.
* Tan-chian English School, 130 Chungsan North Road 2F, Taipei; tel. 541-9089.
* Tan-Ta Language Center, 230 Shinyi Road, Section 2, Taipei; tel. 396-9042.
* Tong-Bau Language Center, 21-1 Chunghsian North Road 3F, Section 2, Taipei; tel. 542-0220/1504.
* Wai-Hsing Language Center, 12 Roosevelt Road 2F, Section 2, Taipei; tel. 394-8088.
* Weg English School, 402 Tunhua South Road, Taipei; tel. 731-3095/3098.
* Wei-Jen Private School, 192 Chunghua Road, Taipei; tel. 361-0670/0678.
* Wu-Chou Language Center, 55 Chungking South Road 3F, Section 1, Taipei; tel. 331-1021.
* Yan-chi English School, 199 Hsinyi Road 3F, Lane 199, Section 4, Taipei; tel. 700-5163/5265.
* YMCA, 9 Hsuchang Street, Taipei; tel. 381-4727-9.
* YMCA, 290 Kunming Street, Taipei; tel. 314-3757-8.
* YMCA, 214 Roosevelt Road, Section 3, Taipei; tel. 365-4849/50.
* YMCA, 500 Yungchi Road, Taipei; tel. 763-1261-3.
* Yo-Lien English School, 291 Hsinyi Road 3F, Section 4, Taipei; tel. 776-2878. Business English.
* Yo-Shing-Shin English Center, 7 Nanking West Road 3F, Taipei; tel. 522-1271.

## UNIVERSITIES

* Chinese Cultural University, Department of English (CTVCE), 41 Chunghsiao East Road, Section 1, Taipei; tel. 916-1758.
* Chingi University, English Department, 72 Chunghsiao West Road, Section 1, Taipei; tel. 311-4595. Also 163 Hsiangshang South Road, Section 1, Taichung; tel. 04-389-4030.
* Fuchien University, Department of English, 510 Chungchun Road, Hsinchuang City (Taipei); tel. 903-1111.
* Shi-da (National Normal) University, English Department, 129-1 Hoping East Road, Section 1, Taipei; tel. 321-8457.

## OTHER CITIES

* Dai-Cho-Tsun Language School, 105 Chungcheng Road 6F, Taichung; also 84 Sanmin Road, Section 3, Taichung; tel. 04-228-2458 (Taichung) or 02-567-0765 (Taipei). Large school with branches throughout Taiwan.
* Join Me Language School, 104 Kuokuang Road 2F, Taichung; tel. 04-226-7597/8. Features classes for mothers and children.
* Join Me Language School, 189 Gansu Road, Section 1, Taichung; tel. 04-323-3486.
* Jordan Language School, Kuangfu Road, Taichung; tel. 04-227-2373.
* Maike Foreign Language School, 97-2 Nantun Road, Section 1, Taichung; tel. 04-376-0071.
* New World Language School, 137 Luchuan West Street 8F, Taichung; tel. 04-223-0650.
* Taipei Language Institute, 16 Lane 118, Chin Hua N. Rd., Taichung; tel. 04-231-8842.
* The Way Language School, Luchuan East Street #32 11F, Taichung; tel. 04-224-2850.
* Taipei Language Institute, 37 Chunghua 3rd Rd., Kaohsiung; tel. 07-251-3638.

## *A QUICK GUIDE TO ENGLISH GRAMMAR*

Only the most perverse academicians actually enjoy studying grammar. Nevertheless, if you're serious about preparing for your English classroom, you'll take a few hours to study--*really* study--this overview. By doing so, you'll save yourself a lot of embarrassment when your students inevitably ask you to explain why a sentence has to be the way it is. Explaining "it just is" will certainly lower the student's opinion of you as a teacher whereas a succinct explanation using the information below will make you seem like a pro.

You may want to use the following description of English grammar as a good sequencing of grammatical structures for presentation to your foreign students. A student's level of proficiency can also be judged somewhat by determining what structures he or she is proficient with. Try to be sure all earlier structures are fairly well mastered before moving on to more advanced grammar.

### *"Be"* verb:

An irregular verb which changes depending on person and number.

Singular: 1st=*I am,* 2nd=*You are,* 3rd=*He/She/It is.*

Plural: 1st=*We are,* 2nd=*You are,* 3rd=*They are.*

Used for occupations, nationality, age, characteristics, condition, size or shape, color or place.

Placed at the beginning of the sentence to form yes-no questions.

Past tense: *was/were* depending on person and number.

Follows *wh-* words in information questions that ask *who* (person), *what* (thing), *where* (place), *when* (time) or *why* (reason).

Used with nominative pronouns *I, you, he/she/it, we, they.* Such pronouns require a referent person or thing before use.

Can be contracted using apostrophes to indicate missing letters to *I'm, you're, he's/she's/its, we're, they're, that's who's, what's, where's, here's, there's.*

Can be negated into *isn't, wasn't, aren't, weren't.*

## Demonstratives:

*This* (singular) and *these* (plural) refer to objects close to the speaker.

*That* (singular) and *those* (plural) refer to objects some ways from speaker.

May be used in noun position or as adjectives before nouns.

## Place words:

*Here* indicates the speaker's location. *There* indicates a place which can be pointed to or which has been previously mentioned.

## Articles:

Most singular nouns are preceded by *a* if the following word begins with a consonant sound and *an* if the following word begins with a vowel.

*The* is used for singular nouns and indicates a specific item, as contrasted with the more general *a.*

## Names and Titles:

No title is used before a given name if the family name is not mentioned.

A man may be called *Mr.* when his given and last names are mentioned or only his last name. He may also sometimes be called by his last name without his title but this is considered either highly impersonal (as in military or police usage) or very "chummy." Recently, some women too are encouraging such usage for themselves to emphasize its sex-neutral implications.

A woman may be called *Mrs.* with either her husband's or her own given name and usually her husband's last name. On legal documents, she must use her given name. Many modern women prefer to hyphenate their maiden (unmarried) name and their husband's name or, in some cases, use their maiden name only even after she has married. Single women usually use the title *Miss* although some women today, both married and single, use *Ms.* to avoid having their marital status identified.

## Simple present tense:

Doesn't actually express present activity (present progressive does that). Used to express repeated, customary, habitual actions and general truths.

When used with a future time expression (word, phrase or clause), indicates that it is a forthcoming event; e.g. "Bill graduates in June."

## Auxiliary *"do"*:

Usually added to sentence before verb to make negative statements or at beginning of sentence to form yes-no questions. As an auxiliary, it has no meaning of its own and is purely functional. Not to be confused with the meaningful *do* which means "act upon."

*Does* used in third person singular (*he/she/it*).

Contracted negative forms: *don't, doesn't.*

Follows *wh-* words for informational questions; e.g., *"Where do you ski?"*

May serve as "pro-verb" also if action is unknown; e.g. *"What do you do on weekends?"*

Used in American English with *have* but not in British English; e.g., American: *"Doesn't he have a pencil?"*; British: *"Hasn't he a pencil?"*

## S-forms *(-s):*

Used after singular nouns and demonstratives and after pronouns *he, she, it.* Simple forms without *-s* are used in all other cases.

## Object pronouns:

Receives the action in a sentence; e.g., *"She kissed me."*

Singular: 1st person=*me*, 2nd=*you*, 3rd=*him/her/it*; Plural: 1st=*us*, 2nd=*you*, 3rd=*them*.

It is used for ships and countries (except in literature) and babies and animals when the sex is unknown.

*Whom* is seldom used in conversation except when it directly follows a preposition; e.g., *"For whom do the bells toll?"* More common and acceptable would be, *"Who do the bells toll for?"* Both are correct.

## Compound sentences:

*And* joins two affirmative statements; e.g., *"Bill eats downtown and watches the people."* Unrelated statements cannot be joined by *and*.

*But* joins contrasting statements, both affirmative and negative; e.g., *"Bill eats downtown but shops at the mall."*

Semicolon (;) is used to join two simple statements instead of *and* or *but;* e.g., *"Bill eats downtown; he shops at the mall."* A comma must never be used this way.

## Phrases:

A group of words which function together as a unit to perform a single function, filling a position in a sentence pattern.

Does not have a subject and related verb.

## Prepositional phrases:

Usually introduced by a preposition, especially when describing a place; e.g. *in a library, at the movies.*

Two or more place phrases may be used together; e.g., *on a table down the hall.* Usually appear at the end of a sentence but may be placed at the beginning for emphasis, generally with the expletive *there;* e.g., *"At the park, there are swans."*

Verbs of motion *(go, walk, etc.)* are often followed by place phrases beginning with *to;* e.g., *"I'll go to the park."* Some places require use of *to,* an article and the place. Others don't require the article; e.g. *"We go to school."* Still others (such as home and downtown) require neither; e.g., *"You go home."*

Time phrases are similar to place phrases and take prepositions *in, at,* and *on;* e.g. *"in the morning," "at noon,"* and *"on Sundays."* (The *-s* with Sunday indicates a habitual action.) Usually appear at the end of a sentence but may also be placed at the end for emphasis. Time phrases with *every* do not use a preposition; e.g., *"every Sunday."*

## Two-word verbs:

Phrases consisting of a verb and a particle (preposition or adverb) which changes the meaning of the verb. The two words function together and cannot be taken separately without changing the meaning of the verb; e.g., *get up* (from bed).

## Voiced/voiceless sounds:

Voiced sounds are made with the vocal cords vibrating, voiceless without; e.g., *f, p, t,* and *k.* All vowels are voiced and half of all consonants.

## Continuous present tense:

Also called present progressive.

Formed by joining present form of auxiliary *be* plus a simple verb plus an *-ing* form.

Used to express action occurring in immediate present *("I am eating")* or for actions or conditions during a period of time including the present; e.g., *"He's studying English this month."*

May also be used to indicate a forthcoming event; e.g., *"He's graduating in June."*

When used in yes-no questions, contracted form is almost always used; e.g., *"Aren't you going to eat?"* The uncontracted form is more formal and

requires the *not* to be placed directly before the
–*ing* form; *"Are you not going to eat?"*

Usually reserved for action verbs. Non-action
verbs which express mental states or conditions and
verbs of perception don't usually use continuous
present; e.g., *believe, know, seem, understand, like,
love, need, prefer, want, wish, remember, forget,
belong, own, owe, cost, mean, resemble, hear, see.*

## –ing-forms:

Depending on function, also called present
participle, gerund, verbal, verbal noun, verbal
adjective.

Spelling rules when adding –*ing:* when simple
verb ends in *e,* drop *e* before adding –*ing.* When
one-syllable verb ends in a single consonant,
preceded by single vowel (e.g., *stop),* double
consonant before adding –*ing.* If preceded by two
vowels (e.g., *look),* do not double consonant (e.g.,
*looking).*

Never functions alone as a verb; e.g. *"I trying
to study."* Always requires the auxiliary be in one
of its conjugated forms (e.g., *is, am, are).*

## Expletive *"there":*

Not an adverb denoting a place, in this usage,
it is a word which means nothing but calls attention
to whatever is referred to in the rest of the
sentence.

Usually followed by *be* verb.

Agrees in number (singular or plural) with
subject which follows it.

Usually requires a place expression for
completion; e.g. *"There are two books on the table."*
A place expression is required even if it is the
place, *there;* e.g., *"There's a book there."*

Sentence pattern is normal if there refers to
a place already mentioned; e.g., *"There a student
can study freely."* Sentence pattern is inverted if
there refers to something being pointed to; e.g.,
*"There is my book." Here* functions the same way.

## Possessive pronouns:

May either modify nouns (e.g., *my, your, his/her/its, our, their*) or be used in place of nouns; e.g., *mine, yours, his/hers/its, ours, theirs.*

When used in place of nouns, they must refer to something recently mentioned; e.g., *"That book is mine. Where's yours?"*

*Whose* is the possessive form of *who.* It usually appears directly before a noun; e.g. *"Whose dog is this?"* It can also be used by itself but only if the items possessed are in sight and indicated; e.g. *"Whose is this?"*

## Frequency Adverbs:

Used to express approximately how often a customary or habitual action or condition is repeated.

Not usually used with continuous tenses; e.g. *is going.*

Include (in declining frequency): Affirmatives: *always, usually, frequently, often, sometimes, occasionally.* Negatives: *seldom, rarely, hardly ever, never.* Interrogative: *Ever?*

Immediately precede the verb in simple statements unless verb is *be* in which case they follow; *"He often calls his mother," "He is always concerned."* Sometimes also may appear at sentence beginning and end.

Affirmative forms used to negate with *not.* Negative forms alone also negate; e.g. *"He doesn't often forget." "He seldom forgets."*

## Numbers:

Cardinal numbers are used in counting and reckoning (math).

Ordinal numbers indicate rank; e.g., *"first place."*

When a noun is modified by both a cardinal and ordinal number, the ordinal number comes first; e.g. *"The first ten days of school are the most difficult."*

Dates are written with cardinal numbers but pronounced as ordinal; e.g., *"July 4, 1776"* is read, *"July fourth, seventeen seventy six."*

## Prepositions used with times, dates and places:

In is used before months, years, seasons, special time expressions (e.g., *"in the evening")*, continents, countries, states, cities and towns.

*On* is used before days of the week, dates, and streets.

*At* is used before the time of day, special time expressions (e.g., *"at night")* and numbers of buildings (e.g., *"He lives at 2728 Elm St.")*

## Transitive/intransitive verbs:

Transitive verbs are those verbs that take an object and are frequently action verbs; e.g. *"He hit the ball."*

Intransitive verbs are frequently "state of being" verbs; e.g., *"He lives in Tokyo."*

## Countables and uncountables:

Uncountables are words for things which cannot be counted; e.g. weather.

Countables must be preceded by *a* or *an* for the singular. Uncountables have no plural forms and can never be preceded by *a* or *an.*

There are four categories of uncountables: abstract (e.g., *advice, help, information, knowledge, trouble, work, enjoyment, fun, recreation, relaxation)*, material (e.g., *meat, rice, bread, cake, coffee, water, oil, grass, hair)*, generic (e.g., *fruit, equipment, furniture, mail, luggage, jewelry, clothing, money)* and non-plurals with final *-s* (e.g., *economics, mathematics, mumps, measles, news, tennis)*.

*A little* and *some* are used before uncountables to indicate a small quantity.

*Much* may be used to indicate large quantities but is mainly used in negative statements and questions; e.g., *"Do you have much work?"*

*A few* is used before plural countables in affirmative statements and questions to indicate a small amount.

*Many* may be used before all plural countables to indicate a large quantity.

*Of* follows *many, much, a few, a little* and *some* when the nouns they modify are identified; e.g., *"Many of my best friends are the students I teach."*

Quantity terms used with both uncountables and plurals: *some* (not usually used in negative statements), *any* (used in negative statements but does not make it negative; e.g., *"I don't use any sugar"), a lot/lots of, no* (indicates an absence; e.g. *no charge.*) *Quite* reverses the meaning of these; e.g. *"quite a few"*= many. *Any* is also used to mean it doesn't matter which or who; e.g., *"Any tourist may enter Osaka castle."*

Verbs used with uncountables are always singular. Pronouns which substitute for uncountables are also singular; e.g. *"Virtue is its own reward."*

Some words may be either countable or uncountable with different meaning depending on which is used; e.g., *change* (alteration or money), *glass* (receptacle or material), *youth* (young person or being young).

Irregular plural countables: *feet, teeth, mice, men, women, children, oxen.*

Some Greek and Latin countables have their original plurals; e.g., *analyses, bases, crises, data, phenomena, stimuli, formulae, media, memoranda.*

No plural form exists for: *deer, fish,* or *sheep.*

Names of some things composed of two similar parts are always plural; e.g., *scissors, tweezers, tongs, trousers, pants, pajamas, glasses, spectacles, binoculars.*

## Reflexive pronouns:

Used with some verbs to emphasize that the subject and object have the same referent; e.g., *"We enjoyed ourselves."*

Used to emphasize that the verb was performed by the subject and not another agent; *"She made lunch herself."*

When preceded by *by,* it means alone (*"Nigel studies by himself."*) or without assistance; e.g., *"He did all the homework by himself."*

## Idioms with *"go"*:

*Go +ing* form of verb is used for active recreation; e.g. *go fishing, go dancing, go skiing.*

## Simple future tense:

Formed with either *be + going to + simple verb;* e.g., *"Judy is going to have a party"* or with *will + simple verb;* e.g. *"Judy will have a party."*

*Will + simple verb* also may suggest promise, determination or inevitability.

For reference to immediate future (just after speaking), use *be + about to + simple verb;* e.g., *"Susan is about to serve the ice cream."*

## Continuous future:

Formed with *will + be + -ing* form; e.g., *"Jack will be helping Judy at her party."*

Used to emphasize an ongoing activity at a very specific time in the future which must be referenced in the sentence or very recently in another sentence.

## Future time expressions:

May be formed with words (e.g., *soon, later, tomorrow*); phrases (e.g., *next (week), in (a minute), (a week) from now* [end of phrase only], *the (day) after (tomorrow), at (noon);* or clauses (groups of words which function as units in a sentence).

Clauses are introduced by "clause markers" (e.g., *where, when, who)* which indicate a clause beginning. Clauses also have subjects which can sometimes be the clause marker; e.g., *"Everyone who sees Kyoto wants to stay."*

Time clauses are introduced by *when; "He will answer when you call."* They may also appear at the beginning of the sentence; e.g., *"When you call, he will answer."* Time clauses always take *-s* form verbs (present tense), never future verbs with *will* or *going.*

## *"Then":*

Can be a time word referring to a time previously mentioned. Usually comes at the end of a sentence; e.g., *"Jeff will be in class then."*

Can also be a sequence signal, like *next,* at the beginning of a sentence; e.g., *"First Pat will eat lunch. Then she'll study."*

*Then* is not a connective to join sentences but is frequently joined by a connective; e.g., *"First Pat will eat lunch and then she'll study."*

## Indefinite *"you"* and *"they":*

In this sense, *you* means anyone or everyone in a colloquial expression; e.g., *"You never know."*

*They* refers to an indefinite body of experts or popular opinion; e.g., *"They say the price of oil will rise."*

## Possessives:

Not all nouns have possessive forms. If not, *of* must be used; e.g. *"legs of the table."*

Nouns with possessive forms include persons, animals, places, times, and money (when followed by worth); e.g., *"five dollars worth of gas."*

When the base form ends in *s,* form the possessive by adding an apostrophe. Otherwise, add apostrophe *s ('s).*

## Adjective phrases:

Consist of a preposition, noun and other modifiers.

Occurs after word it modifies; e.g., *"A boy with green shoes."* Single word adjectives occur before the word; e.g., *"A tall boy..."*

The verb of the sentence agrees in number with the subject noun not with the noun in the adjective phrase; *"That book of wonderful stories about kings, queens, knights and dragons is great!"*

When the adjective phrase limits the meaning of the modified noun to one possibility, the noun is preceded by *the;* e.g., *"The men in that car are suspicious."*

## Simple past tense:

Expresses a one-time completed past event; *"Jerry saw Mary."*

Regular past tense forms end in *-ed.* The approximately 150 irregular forms must be memorized because they are not predictable.

Irregular forms are made by: same as present (e.g., *split, bet*), final consonant change *(built, spent),* vowel and consonant change *(brought, taught),* vowel changes *(bleed=bled, spin=spun, find=found).*

In sentences which require use of auxiliaries, past tense is applied to the auxiliary, not the main verb; e.g., *"Did Hilary walk to school yesterday?"*

*Ago* is used only with simple past tense and appears at the end of the time phrase. It refers to a specific time, counting back from the present; e.g., *"Bill sold his car a week ago."*

*Before* and *after* express a simple sequence relationship; e.g., *"Bill sold his car before he moved."*

*While* emphasizes the passage of time and simultaneous action; *"Emily slept while the teacher lectured."*

Frequently used with continuous tenses (*-ing* form verbs) because of duration; e.g., *"While the teacher was lecturing, Emily slept."*

*When* can refer to punctual action; e.g., *"Where were you when I fell down?"*

## Was/were going to + simple verb:

Expresses unfulfilled plans.

Often followed by *but* and an independent clause (one with subject and verb) explaining why the plan was abandoned; e.g., *"Ted was going to watch TV but he fell asleep."*

### *"One of":*

Introduces a noun phrase which includes a plural noun.

The plural noun is always modified; e.g., *"one of my students."*

When the *"one of"* phrase is the subject of a clause, the verb form is singular. It agrees with *one;* e.g., *"One of the boys was late."*

The possessive *of* is used to avoid ambiguity; e.g., *"at the home of one of my friends."*

*None of* is similar but it requires the verb to agree with noun following *of* if the phrase is the subject of a clause; e.g., *"None of the teachers want to grade homework."*

### *"In, on, at"* (continued):

*In* indicates the position of something surrounded; e.g., *"in the library."*

*On* indicates contact with a surface; e.g., *"on the table."*

*At* indicates proximity; e.g., *"the girl at the window."*

### *Used to* + verb:

Expresses past custom, habit or repeated action which no longer occurs; e.g., *"I used to go bowling."*

Questions and negatives are formed with the auxiliary *do* as in the simple past.

### *Any more:*

An adverbial expression used in negative statements and questions indicating that a condition or situation which previously existed no longer exists; e.g., *"I don't go bowling any more."*

## *Have to* + verb:

Expresses necessity. Uses auxiliary *do* for questions and negatives; *"Do you have to go home now?"*

May be affirmative (e.g., *"We have to eat every day"*), negative (*"But people who fast don't have to eat every day"*), yes-no questions (e.g., *"Do we have to study every day?"*) or information questions (e.g., *"When do we have to leave for the show?"*)

## Expletive *it:*

In this sense, *it* fills a position in the sentence and doesn't refer to anything; e.g., *"It won't take long to finish."*

May be used as impersonal *it* for weather, time, distance and identification (e.g., *"Who is it?"*)

## *Very, too, enough:*

*Very* is an intensifier which strengthens the word which immediately follows; *"Debbie was very kind."* Precedes the word it modifies.

*Too* does not intensify and is more specific than *very*. Used when an action is impossible because of the condition following *too; "It was too nice outside to work."* Sometimes used for great difficulty rather than impossibility; e.g., *"He talks too fast to understand."* Precedes the word it modifies.

*Enough* means a sufficiency. Used when the infinitive after *enough* is made possible by the situation before *enough; "Ken was smart enough to go to Stanford."* Follows the word it modifies. (Infinitives are units with *to* and a simple verb; e.g., *to go.)*

## Duration:

Duration of a condition or activity may be expressed with *for* and *until.*

*For* introduces a phrase. Often followed by a cardinal number or *a; e.g. "for seven days."*

*Until* introduces a phrase or clause. The time stated indicates the end of the duration period; *"Jim works until five o'clock."*

## Continuous past tense:

Formed by a verb phrase made of a past form of *be* and an *-ing* form; e.g., *was walking.* Patterns are same as those of continuous present.

Sometimes called past progressive tense.

Requires use with expression of specific time (either in sentence or recently referred to in earlier sentence). Time expression may occur at the beginning or end of the sentence; e.g., *"Jeff was painting his apartment all day."*

Frequently used with *while.*

## Compound sentences:

Two whole, complete sentences joined together by a connective (e.g., *and, but,* etc.) to form one sentence with different subjects but only one predicate (verb).

The second predicate is reduced to the first auxiliary of the verb phrase in continuous tenses (*be* + *-ing* form); e.g., *"Claire was reading a book and Jack was too."* (Reading is implied for Jack's action.)

*Do* is used instead of the auxiliary if the first verb is in simple present or past form; e.g., *"Sam studies hard and Jun does too."* *Do* is also used to replace *used to* and *have to; "Julie had to leave early and Louise did too."*

*Too* is used when statements are affirmative; *either* is used for negative statements; e.g., *"Claire didn't leave the library and Jack didn't either."*

*So* and *neither* may be used instead of *too* and *either* but must be placed immediately following the connective and cause the word order of the second clause to be inverted; e.g., *"Tony didn't visit Korea and neither did Karen."*

### *Each/every/all:*

*Each* focuses on the separate members of a group; e.g., *"Each student must submit a report."*

*Every,* emphasizes the unity and commonality of the group; e.g., *"Every student wants to do well."*

*All* stresses completeness and finality. It is used before plurals and uncountables. The verb form agrees with the noun which follows all; e.g., *"All [of] the flowers were displayed beautifully."* (*Of* is optional.)

*Not all* means part; e.g., *"Not all artists display their works."*

### *"One"* as a non-number:

May be an indefinite personal pronoun meaning any or every person. Rather formal and usually used only in writing; e.g., *"One must be diligent."*

May be used to avoid repetition of lengthy noun phrases; e.g., *"Our school has a three-month summer vacation but not every school has one."*

### *"Other"* as an adjective and pronoun:

As an adjective, may be either *another* in front of singular nouns or *other* before plurals and uncountables; e.g. *"other languages."*

May replace singular nouns with *another* and plural nouns with other; e.g., *"One farmer was planting, another was sowing, the others were watching the harvest."* The other/s refer to the remaining one/s in a group.

### *How questions:*

May be answered by *by + noun* for questions pertaining to transportation or communication. The noun is a simple form with no article or modifier; e.g., *"How did you get here? I got here by car."*

May be answered by *by + ing* form for questions about action; e.g.; *"How do you speak in front of a group? By practicing."*

May be answered by *with + noun* for questions about instrument, equipment, or method used; e.g., *"How did you fix the stereo? With a hammer."*

May be answered with a single adjective when asking about the description of an object; e.g., *"How do you like your coffee? Black."* When a complete sentence is used to respond, the adjective is placed at the end of the sentence; e.g.; *"I like my coffee black."*

How questions about manner require *-ly* adverbs; e.g., *"How do you feed a mountain lion? Carefully."*

## How question phrases:

*How* followed by an adjective or a term of quantity, time, manner, distance or frequency; e.g., *"How old is Hideo?"*

How phrases serve as a unit to act as a question word in an information question pattern; e.g., *"How long ago did Erika leave?"* = *"When did Erika leave?"*

Answers to *how often* may be frequency adverbs or time phrases; e.g., *"How often do you go downtown? Every weekend."*

## Adverbs of manner:

Usually formed by adding *-ly* to related adjectives: *quick = quickly.*

Irregular manner adverbs do not end in *-ly* and are the same as their adjective equivalents. These include *hard,* and *fast* and sometimes *slow.* *Well* is the adverbial form of the adjective *good.* As an adjective, *well* refers to a person's health.

They are never placed between a verb and its object; e.g., *"I hit the ball hard."*

## Questions with *"what, which, whose"*:

Often followed by nouns to form questions similar to *how* questions; e.g. *"What time did Sumi leave?"*

*What kind of* is used to question sort, style, make, type, color, flavor, and size. *Of* is not used to answer questions of color, flavor or size; e.g., *"What color car do you have?"*

Causative constructions:

Sentence pattern with two verbs which explain how one person causes another person to do something.

Used with the causative verbs *have, make and get.*

*Have* suggests the person acted upon is in the employ of the actor; *"Jan had the mechanic check her* brakes."

*Make* suggests use of some kind of force or coercion; e.g., *"Teachers often make bad students do more homework."*

*Get* usually suggests persuasion; e.g., *"I got my best friend to lend me ten dollars."*

The causative verb is inflected (i.e., changed). The action verb is in simple form with *make* or *have;* e.g., *"The mailman made me go to the post office for my package." "While I was there, I had the clerk check the regulations."*

The action verb is an infinitive form with *get;* e.g., *"Danny got his mother to clean his room every day."*

*Let* and *help* function like causatives. *Let* is like *have* and *make.*

*Help* may be formed with an infinitive when the actor is a modifying clause; e.g., *"The driver helped the students who came late to find the classroom."*

"Get used to" and "be used to":

Idioms that deal with becoming or being accustomed to a situation; e.g., *"Diane is getting used to a small apartment." "Takeshi still isn't used to American accents but he understands more now than he used to."*

Not to be confused with *used to + simple verb* which suggests a past habit; e.g. *"He used to smoke."*

## Appositives:

Construction in which two words or phrases are next to each and identify the same object or person, with the second usually modifying the first; e.g., *"Mr. Kan, the new dean, seems to be a fine man."*

## By (a time period):

Used to refer to an activity which requires an indefinite but considerable length of time before completion. Completion may take place at or before the time mentioned; e.g., *"I'll speak fluent Japanese by the turn of the century--the 22nd!"*

## Present perfect tense:

Made from present form of auxiliary *have* and the past participle of a verb. All but about fifty verbs have regular past participle forms ending in *-en.*

Auxiliary *have* is identical to the verb *have* except that the auxiliary joins with pronouns and contracts more readily than the verb; *"He's gotten all A's this year."* Negative contractions are *haven't, hasn't, hadn't.*

Used to indicate an action or state which was repeated in the past and which may be repeated in the future (e.g., *"I have eaten sushi."*); an action or state completed at some unspecified past time (usually includes *just, already, recently* and, if negative, *yet: "I haven't seen Sapporo yet"*); or an action or state which began some time in the past and has continued to the moment of speaking (usually includes *for* or *since ("Bill's studied "kendo" since 1988").*

## "Just, recently, already, yet":

Often occur between the auxiliary and main verb, like frequency adverbs. *Just* must occur here (e.g., *"Kimi has just seen an old friend"*), the others may occur at the end of a sentence; *"She's talked to her already."*

*Yet* is used only in questions and negative statements and always occurs at the end of a sentence; e.g., *"She hasn't told her about school yet."*

*Just* means immediately before speaking. *Recently* means a short while ago. *Already* suggests an action sooner than was expected (e.g., *"He knows "hangul" already"*). *Yet* suggests a time later than expected (e.g., *"But he hasn't learned the subway system yet"*).

## Continuous present perfect tense:

Phrases are made of a present form of auxiliary *have + been + -ing* form.

Time expressions using *for* or *since* or expressions of recent time (e.g., *this week, today)* are required; *"Douglas been reading "War and Peace" since 1985."*

Emphasizes duration and implies that the action will continue.

## Simple past perfect tense:

A verb phrase consisting of auxiliary *have +* a past participle.

Used to express time between two events in the past; e.g., *"Sam had talked to Sony on the phone many times before he interviewed with them."*

Used to report statements in the simple past or present perfect (reported speech); e.g., *"Rita said that she had lost her wallet."*

Used to express wishes or unreal conditions about the past; e.g., *"She wishes that she hadn't gone."*

## Continuous past perfect tense:

A verb phrase consisting of auxiliary *had + been + ing form.*

Used to express duration of a past event that was interrupted or concluded by another event; e.g.,

*"Greg had been waiting for an hour when the train finally arrived."*

Simple past perfect may be used with little difference in meaning; e.g., *"Greg had waited..."* = *"Greg waited..."*


Indirect objects:

Usually a person to whom or for whom something is done.

May be preceded by *to, for,* or *neither.*

Position in sentence varies according to whether it is introduced by a proposition and the nature of the direct object.

If no preposition, the indirect object precedes the direct object; e.g., *"Carol asked the student her name."*

If used with *to* or *for,* the indirect object follows the direct object; e.g., *"The student told her name to Carol."* If the direct object is a clause, the indirect object precedes it; e.g., *"Carol told the girl that she was glad to meet her."*

## *"Say, tell, talk, speak":*

*Say* used usually to introduce a direct or indirect quotation; e.g., *"Aya said, "I want to learn English well."*

*Tell* usually requires an indirect object and is rarely used for direct quotations; e.g. *"Janice told Ed how to get to the store."*

*Talk* usually refers to a conversation. There is no direct object but it sometimes has an indirect object after *to;* e.g., *"Students can't talk during a test."*

*Speak* can mean *to speak* when it is followed by *to* and an indirect object; e.g., *"A good teacher always speaks to her students when she sees them outside of class."* An alternative meaning is to address in a formal fashion; e.g., *"Dan spoke at the commencement."*

## Noun clauses:

Most often introduced by connective *that* with *say* or *tell*. Frequently omitted in spoken form; *"George said [that] he was sorry to be late."*

*Ask* is used to place a question and never is followed by a *that* clause. It may have a clause object introduced by *if;* e.g., *"The students asked if that meant there would be no test today."*

## Simple future perfect tense:

Made from *will + have + past participle.*

Used to relate the completion of an act or condition before another action or time in the future.

Must include a future time expression, usually *when* clauses or phrases introduced by *in, next* or *by;* e.g., *"By Thursday, the doctor will have treated forty patients."*

## Continuous future perfect tense:

Made from *will + have + been + ing* form.

Emphasizes the duration of a future event or present situation which reaches into the future.

Two time expressions are required, one as a specific time or event and the other as the duration: e.g., *"When Harumi goes to America, she will have been studying English for many years."*

Simple future perfect tense frequently used instead; e.g., *"When Harumi goes to America, she will have studied English for many years."*

## Transitive/intransitive verbs:

Transitive verbs may take direct objects; intransitive can not.

Some transitive two-word verbs do not allow objects to occur between the words of the verb. They are inseparable; e.g., *"Deborah called on her aunt today."*

Separable two-word verbs permit (and sometimes require) the object between the words.

Short noun objects (including pronouns) may occur between the parts of a two-word verb or after the verb; e.g., *"He called his friend up." = "He called him up." = "He called up his friend."*

*Right* sometimes modifies two-word verbs to indicate an immediate action; *"Each morning at 6, Tom wakes right up."*

## Tag questions:

Short yes-no questions added to statements.

Used to keep conversation continuation or for confirmation of statement; e.g., *"You didn't really leave, did you?"*

When the statement is affirmative, the question is negative; e.g., *"You told him, didn't you?"*

When the statement is negative, the question is affirmative; e.g., *"You didn't tell him, did you?"*

The verb in the question is the first auxiliary of the verb phrase; e.g., *"Bob hasn't seen Sam, has he?"*

If the verb in the statement is a single form of any verb except *be,* the verb in the question is that same form of *do;* e.g., *"You told him didn't you?"* This is also true when the verb is *used to* or *have to;* e.g., *"Sally had to stay late, didn't she?"*

The second word of the tag question must be the subject form of a personal pronoun (e.g., *he, she,* etc.) or expletives *it* or *there;* e.g., *"Learning Korean is hard, isn't it?"*

## Modal auxiliaries (modals):

Unlike other auxiliaries (*do, be, have),* modals have no *-s form, -ing form* or participles.

Comprised of *can/could, will/would, shall/should/ought, may/might,* and *most.*

Form of the modal does not necessarily indicate the time reference of the sentence. For example, the "past" form (e.g., *could)* can express the same meaning as *can.* Also, negated modals (e.g., *couldn't)* don't always mean the opposite of affirmative ones.

Rules are somewhat imprecise. Memorization of usage is advised.

*Can* suggests ability, possibility, opportunity or permission in present ability; e.g., *"Elliot can dance like John Travolta."*

*Could* suggests past ability with possibly a changed condition; e.g., *"Until yesterday, Jill could ride free with her pass."* Also suggests present or future impossibility; *"Jim could go to the beach if he didn't have class."*

*Can* or *could* suggest future possibility; e.g., *"The doctor can see you at 2 p.m."*

*Could have + past participle* suggests past opportunity not realized; e.g., *"The driver could have stopped before the patch of ice."* [Implication: he didn't.] Past opportunity realized cannot be expressed with a modal. (It just happened!)

*Couldn't have + past participle* infers past impossibility; e.g., *"I'm sorry he couldn't have seen you yesterday."*

Present or future permission is expressed with *can* or *may;* e.g., *"You may leave now," "You can leave at 3 p.m."*

*Could* or *might* indicates past permission with suggestion of changed condition; e.g., *"Before the new government, no one could vote in Russia."* *Might* is an older form; *could* is more widely used.

*Will* is used for a future plan, promise or agreement; e.g., *"I will finish my homework by 7 so we can go out."*

*Will + be + ing* form suggests a continuing future activity; *"The prime minister will be meeting with his cabinet tomorrow."*

*Will + have + past participle* suggests completion of a future activity; e.g.; *"Jessie will have driven 1,000 miles by sunset."*

*Will* and *would* are used to make a polite request for future action; e.g., *"Will/would you fix me a cup of tea?"* *Would* may be somewhat more polite.

*Would* is used for present and past contrary-to-fact statements; *"If Jack hadn't hurt himself, he'd be captain of the team by now."* (Note contracted form of *would.*)

*Shall/should/ought* express advisability, obligation, expectation and chance.

*Shall* or *should* are used in affirmative questions of advisability; e.g., *"Shall we go to the beach?"*

*Should* may be used for negative questions of advisability (e.g., *"Shouldn't we be doing our homework?"* [Implication: we aren't.]) or chance happenings; e.g., *"If you should go by the store, could you get me some milk?"*

*Should* or *ought* are used for statements of advisability (e.g., *"You ought to be careful with appliances"*), for unfulfilled obligations (e.g., *"I should be studying but 'Cops 'n Bloopers' is on TV."* Fulfilled obligations can not be expressed with a modal) and expectation or likelihood (e.g., *"The guests should be arriving soon."*)

*May* is used for present or future permission; e.g., *"You may leave now" "You may leave at 2."* Past permission can not be expressed with a modal.

*May* or *might* is used for present or future situations of conjecture (e.g., *"He may be at the park."*).

*May* or *might + be + ing* form is used for conjecture about a present activity; e.g., *"Ed might be watching TV."*

Conjecture about the past is done with *may/might + have + past participle*; e.g., *"I might have left my notebook on the subway."*

*Must* suggests necessity (e.g., *"I must go."*), abstention (e.g., *"We must not be quick to judge."*) or deduction.

Lack of necessity (past and present) is not expressed with a modal because *must* has no past form. *Have to* is used instead; e.g., *"Bill doesn't have to leave the country for his visa."*

Deduction about a present situation is done using *must + simple verb* or *must + be + -ing form*; *"Our mailman must work hard. He must be delivering a thousand letters today."*

Deduction about the future requires *must + be + going to*; e.g., *"That girl must be going to go to* _a dance."_ Deduction about the past requires _must + have + been;_ e.g., _"Japan must have been dangerous in the samurai era."_

All modals (except _ought)_ are followed by simple verbs. _Ought_ is followed by an infinitive; e.g., _"You really ought to dress better, Sam."_

Adding _not_ after the modal the modal makes a negative.

Like all auxiliaries, questions are made by placing the modal before the subject; e.g., _"Should we go now?"_

Related idioms with modal components may have unrelated meanings; e.g., _can't help, would like, would rather_ (used with _than), had better, maybe, willing._

## Reported speech:

When a sentence relates an indirect quote from the past without literal restating; e.g., _"Jack said that he was jumpy from all the coffee."_ (Direct quote would be, _"Jack said, 'I'm jumpy from all the coffee.'"_)

Reported speech requires the changing of modals from direct to indirect quotation.

_Can_ becomes _could_ (_"The boy said he could jump over"), will = would_ (_"He said he would jump the hedge"), shall = should_ (_"He asked if he should do it"), may = might_ (_"I said he might if he was careful"), must = had to_ (_"He replied that sometimes a boy just had to do what a boy had to do."_)

_Should_ and _ought_ do not change in reported speech; e.g., _"Larry said, "I ought to try it myself." = "He said he ought to try it himself."_

## Imperatives:

Sentence type usually used for giving instructions or making requests (usually with _please_ at beginning or end of the sentence).

Imperatives have no expressed subject and begin with the verb phrase; e.g., _"Get off the bus at Main Street."_

Negative forms may be made as usual or with *never* in the beginning position or with *ever* and a negative verb; e.g., *"Don't ever eat ice cream too fast."* = *"Never eat ice cream too fast."*

## Subjunctive objects:

These are usually phrases of suggestion introduced by a verb phrase beginning with *that;* e.g., *"Danielle suggested that Bob go to Yale."*

Usually, the tenses of different verbs in the same sentence agree; e.g. *"I know that you agree."* There is no agreement of tense sequence in subjunctive objects because the verb in the clause (after *that*) does not exist at the time of speaking; *"She has often urged that he go someplace prestigious."*

Verbs taking subjunctive noun-clause objects include: *advise, ask, demand, forbid, insist, prefer, propose, recommend, request, require, suggest, urge* (among others).

## Noun-clause objects:

When a clause functions as a direct object, the word order is altered so the verb follows the subject: *"Where is my book?"* = *"Do you know where my book is?"*

Auxiliaries usually precede the subject. In noun clauses, though, they follow the subject; e.g., *"Why is she laughing?"* = *"Do you know why she is laughing?"*

Auxiliary *do* vanishes when changed to a noun clause but the inflection (ending) it had is transferred to the main verb of the noun clause; e.g.; *"Where does Bob go on weekends?"* = *"I wonder where Bob goes on weekends."*

## Infinitive phrases:

Usually a statement, not a question, followed by an *s-form* verb; e.g., *"To learn a foreign language is valuable."*

The infinitive phrase as subject may appear at the end of a sentence if the sentence begins with the anticipatory _it;_ e.g., _"It is very difficult for me to learn one." = "To learn one is very difficult for me."_

Subjects of infinitives appear before the infinitive; e.g., _"Teachers expect students to study."_ (The phrase _"students to study"_ is the direct object of _"teaches expect.")_

In compound sentences, the infinitive is frequently abbreviated to _to_ if the phrases' verb are the same; _"Many young Americans want to visit Asia but many older ones don't want to."_

Infinitives may modify nouns (e.g., _"Clair has a letter to write"),_ adjectives or adverbs (e.g., _"Don't be afraid to fail"),_ verbs (e.g., _"Don't hesitate to ask")_ and compound indefinites (_someone, anyone, anything,_ etc.); e.g., _"There isn't anything to eat in my house."_

Object phrases beginning with question words (_which, why, how,_ etc.) often take infinitives; e.g., _"I can't decide how to teach infinitives." ("how to teach infinitives"_ is the object of _"decide.")_

Imperatives in direct quotes become infinitives in reported speech; e.g., _"Phyllis said, 'Eat a lot, Bill.'" = "Phyllis told Bill to eat a lot."_

## Marked and unmarked adjective clauses:

Each adjective clause has a subject and a verb and modifies the word preceding them; e.g., _"Students who study the hardest succeed the fastest."_ In this example, the clause marker also serves as clause subject.

Most adjective clauses require clause markers to indicate their beginning; e.g. _"I like books that challenge my mind."_ However, unmarked clauses have no clause markers (or may take an optional _which_ or _that),_ making the clauses difficult to recognize; e.g. _"They fill me with thoughts [that] I never had."_

The above adjective clauses are essential for the meaning of their sentences. For this reason, they are called "restrictive adjective clauses."

"Non-restrictive adjective clauses" are frequently set off by commas, are non-essential and may be deleted without affecting the sentence's meaning; e.g., *"Grammar, which can get awfully boring, really is essential."*

## Gerunds:

*-Ing* forms which serve as subjects.

Usually function as uncountables although sometimes a plural ending may be added; e.g., *readings, writings, teachings.*

Verbal in nature since it can take its own subject and object; e.g., *"My failing to explain this material well could cause some confusion."*

Some verbs often take gerunds as objects but won't take infinitives; e.g., *"Jack considers watching TV challenging."* Other verbs will take either a gerund or an infinitive as objects; e.g., *"He prefers concentrating [or to concentrate] on it alone."*

Sense perception verbs (*notice, hear, observe, smell, see, feel, watch*) may take simple or gerund objects but not infinitives; e.g., *"She heard singing in the other room."*

*-ing* form emphasizes on-going action. Simple verbs suggest that the action is finished; e.g., *"She heard someone sing in the other room."* [Implication: *she's not singing now.*]

*Forget* and *remember* may take either a gerund or infinitive object with different meanings. Gerund objects express actions occurring before the main verb; e.g., *"Alan remembers telling Pete he would be absent."* Infinitive objects with *remember* express action after the main verb; e.g., *"Please remember to put out the candle."* With *forget*, infinitive objects express actions which won't or shouldn't occur; e.g., *"Don't forget to extinguish it."*

## *-ing* forms as noun modifiers:

Also called present participles or verbal adjectives.

Appear before nouns to be modified (e.g., *"blinding light,"* *"intriguing premise"*), after a noun to be modified (e.g., *"I find my clothes boring."*) or

after the verb *be* (e.g., *"Driving is frustrating."*)
*-ing* forms in time phrases and after prepositions:

Must be used after time words *before, after, until, since, while* and *when;* e.g., *"Betty shrieked before dropping the dish."* Infinitives may never follow these time words.

Must be used immediately after all prepositions except *to;* e.g., *"Dick planned on going to Bangkok over the holidays."*

Passive voice:

Unlike the usual "active voice," passive voice puts the performer of the action at the end of the sentence or may delete it altogether, putting the object of the action at the beginning; e.g., *"The dish was dropped by Betty."*

Only transitive verbs may be used with the passive voice.

Passive sentences always contain auxiliary *be* and a past participle. Other auxiliaries may precede *be;* e.g., *"Homework must be completed (by all students)."*

Used when the specific performer of the action is unknown (e.g., *"Judy's car was made in Japan"*), when we choose not to mention the performer (e.g., *"Beth was told she would have to repeat the course"*), when we want to emphasize the object (e.g., *"Passports are checked carefully," "Electricity was discovered by Ben Franklin."*)

With *have* in causative constructions, the performer is frequently omitted because it is not important. These constructions are not true passives because they don't contain *be* but they are very similar; e.g., *"The IRS has tax returns sent to local centers."* [What could be less important than us mere taxpayers?]

Past participles used as noun modifiers also are related to passives; *"Trucking is a regulated industry."* [We don't know who regulates.]

## Comparisons:

Complete sameness may be expressed with *the same as* (e.g., *"Bill's Toyota is the same as Susan's."*) or with *alike;* e.g., *"Bill's and Susan's Toyotas are alike."*

Similarity in many respects is indicated with *like;* e.g., *"Phil's teaching style is like Jack's: laid back."*

Similarity in one respect is shown with *the same + noun* (e.g., *"Edgar and Jackie are the same age"*) or with *the same + noun + as;* e.g. *"Edgar is the same age as Jackie (is)"*) or with *as + adj/adv/(many + noun) + as;* e.g., *"George's watercolor was as lovely as Anna's." "I didn't do as many paintings as they did."*

*Almost, nearly,* and *about* limit similarity; e.g., *"Bill's Toyota is almost the same as Susan's." Just* and *exactly* enhance the similarity; *"Phil's teaching style is just like Jack's."*

Statements of difference are formed with *differs from* (e.g., *"Jan's dog differs from Al's in color"*), or *different from;* e.g., *"They're both different from Jack's."*

*Somewhat* and *a little* limit the difference; e.g., *"Jan's dog is somewhat browner than Al's." Quite, very* and *entirely* enhance the difference; e.g., *"They're both entirely different from Jack's."*

## Comparison of two different groups:

If the comparative adjective or adverb ends in *-er,* it will usually be followed by *than.*

One-syllable adjectives and adverbs are made into comparative by merely adding *-er* to the end; e.g., *faster.* If they end in *-y,* the ending is *-ier;* e.g., *happier.*

Similarity in one respect is shown with *the same + noun* (e.g., *"Edgar and Jackie are the same age"),* or with the same + noun + as; e.g., *"Edgar is the same age."*

If adjectives or adverbs have more than two syllables, they usually don't have comparatives. Instead, they take *more* before and *than* after; e.g., _"more beautiful than."_ May also be used with _less_ instead of _more._

Double comparatives are used to express degree to which one characteristic is dependent on another; e.g., _"The faster I run, the 'behinder' I get."_

## Superlatives:

Used to indicate the highest degree of the adjective or adverb in a group of three or more; _"She was the fairest of them all."_

One-syllable superlatives end in _-est._ Adjectives or adverbs ending in _-y_ have superlatives ending in _-iest._ Most adjectives or adverbs with more than two syllables do not have superlatives. Instead, they use the most; _"She was the most beautiful at the ball."_ _Least_ is used as the opposite of _most._

Irregular comparative and superlative forms: _good, better, best; well, better, best; bad, worse, worst; badly, worse, worst; little, less, least; much, more, most; many, more, most; far, farther, farthest._

## Conditional _"if"_ clauses:

Express conditions which may produce the imagined result described in the main clause.

Future conditions are indicated in the present tense; e.g., _"She'll get a good grade if she studies."_

Present conditions are indicated in the past tense. Result phrase includes one of the modals _would, could,_ or _might;_ e.g., _"If Jack ate better, he might lose weight."_

Past conditions are indicated in the past perfect tense (_had_ + past participle) with result clause including _would, could,_ or _might_ and the present perfect tense (_have_ + past participle); e.g., _"I would have come sooner if I'd known you were sick."_

## *"Unless"* conditional clauses:

Have the same form as if clauses but negatives are affirmative and affirmatives are negative; e.g., *"Jack might not lose weight unless he eats better."*

May follow or precede the result clause; e.g. *"Unless he eats better, Jack might not lose weight."*

## *"Whether or not"* clauses:

Indicate that there is no causal relationship between the clauses. May be considered the opposite of *if* clauses.

Very similar to *if* clauses in structure except that *or not* usually appears at the end of the conditional clause; e.g., *"Emma's going to the mountains whether Phil goes or not."* Or not may occur with *whether* if the conditional clause is especially long and possibly confusing; e.g., *"She's driving whether or not Phil decides to help pay for the gas."*

Whether may also suggest alternatives in object clauses (e.g., *"Did Sue say whether she was meeting Paul or Ted tomorrow?)* or in infinitive phrases; e.g., *"She doesn't know whether to go out or stay home?"*

## Use of *"hope"*:

When expressing hope for an unknown something related to self, an infinitive or *that* clause may be used with the same meaning; e.g., *"I hope to go to Taipei soon."* = *"I hope (that) I can go to Taipei soon."*

Only a *that* clause can be used to express hope relating to another person; e.g., *"Sally hopes (that) her students are having a good Christmas."*

Only a present tense may be used to express hope about the unknown present; e.g., *"She hopes (that) they don't forget their English over the holidays."*

Only a past tense may be used to express hope in the unknown past; e.g., *"She hopes (that) they didn't eat too much on New Year's Day."*

Result and reason:

In complex sentences, an independent clause often tells the result of a dependent clause which gives the reason for it.

Reasons are introduced by clause markers which indicate this relationship: *because, as,* and *since* (not time); e.g., *"I went to the gym since my class was canceled."*

This order may be reversed, presenting the reason first. This construction emphasizes the reason over the result and may be considered somewhat more formal; e.g., *"Because Sarah was among the first to arrive, she decided to tour the house."* A pronoun is usually used in the second clause since the noun referent is in the first clause.

Also formal is the use of *thus, therefore, hence, consequently* and *as a result* which do not connect clauses but are used to begin a second sentence; e.g., *"Sarah was among the first to arrive. As a result, she decided to tour the house."* A semicolon with *and* may be used to join the sentences.

*Because of* also is used to express reason; e.g., *"Dan couldn't go hiking because of the bad weather."*

*So* is commonly used to present informally the same reason and result relationship as the formal *thus, hence,* etc.; e.g., *"Sarah arrived early so she practiced reading katakana on the billboards."*

*So* + adj/adv + *that* tells the result of an action caused by the degree of a characteristic; *"Jerry's so ambitious (that) he never has time for friends."* Don't confuse this with *so that* which is used to indicate purpose and contains a modal such as *can, could, will,* or *would;* e.g., *"Jerry is ambitious so (that) he can succeed."* [*That* is frequently omitted in both constructions.]

Purpose is also told by an infinitive and the optional *in order* (e.g., *"Jerry works hard (in order) to succeed"*) or by *for* + noun; e.g, *"He's striving for financial independence."*

*Such/so* + *(modifier* + *noun)* + *that* is a pattern which, like *so* + *adj/adv* + *that,* also gives the result and degree relationship; e.g., *"Japan is such a great country that I want to live there."*

*The reason* + *why/that* + *is that* emphasizes the reason over the result; *"Freddy said the reason (that) he didn't have his assignment was that he had been robbed by pirates."*

*What* at the beginning of a question with *for* at the end means *why; "What did the pirates take his homework for?"* (Because this is a colloquial expression, it defies grammatical explanation. Note preposition *for* at end--now considered acceptable by most grammarians.)

## Concession statements:

Used to indicated unexpected results.

The dependent clause is introduced by *although* and *even though* and may precede or follow the result clause; e.g., *"Even though speaking English is easy for native speakers, foreigners find it very difficult."* = *"Foreigners find speaking English difficult even though it's easy for native speakers."* Notice use of pronoun *it* in second reference (*it = speaking English*).

*In spite of* may be followed by a noun, an –*ing* form or a clause introduced by *the fact that; "In spite of the fact that Janice was late, we got to the show on time."*

*But* at the beginning of a result clause and *anyway* at the end suggests the reason clause is insignificant; e.g., *"The day was cloudy but we had fun at the park anyway."*

*Besides* and *other than* are used to contrast a solitary option; *"John didn't want to visit any place besides Kyoto."* Don't confuse with *beside* (contracted form of *by the side of*).

To contrast a statement just made, *however* is used to relate (but not actually join) sentences; e.g., *"Congratulations! You've just completed your grammar review. However, now you have to explain the stuff to your students!"*